THE BIRD PATH

collected longer poems
1964—1988

THE BIRD PATH
COLLECTED
LONGER
POEMS

KENNETH WHITE

MAINSTREAM
PUBLISHING

The publisher acknowledges subsidy
of the Scottish Arts Council towards
the publication of this volume.

First published in Great Britain in 1989 by
MAINSTREAM PUBLISHING COMPANY (EDINBURGH) LTD
7 Albany Street
Edinburgh EH1 3UG

ISBN 1 85158 2452 (cloth)

British Library Cataloguing in Publication Data

White, Kenneth
The bird path
I. Title
821'.914

ISBN 1-85158-245-2

Typeset in 11 on 12 Garamond by C. R. Barber and Partners
(Highlands) Ltd   Fort William   Scotland
Printed in Great Britain by Billings & Sons Ltd, Worcester

To the memory of
my mother
Janet Downie Cameron
and my father
William Mackenzie White

AUTHOR'S NOTE

The chronology as well as the topology of the whole process having become quite complex, maybe a few words regarding the conception and arrangement of this book will not be out of place.

Of the two early poem-books published in Britain, *The Cold Wind of Dawn* (Jonathan Cape, 1966) and *The Most Difficult Area* (Cape Goliard, 1968), I've chosen to include here, as 'longer' poems, only 'At the Solstice', 'Zone' and 'In Praise of the Rosy Gull' (using this poem as a prelude to the whole 'bird path'). But later I wrote that 'Ballad of Kali Road', which is a kind of Glasgow oratorio, taking up again some *Cold Wind* songs, so it also goes in here. As to 'Ovid's Report', written later again, it was, via the Latin poet, a summing-up of my situation and perspectives at that juncture, so it likewise goes into this opening section.

Thereafter, since the books that followed were published on the Continent and were not readily available to English-language readers, what starts out as a 'Selected longer poems' becomes to all intents and purposes a 'Collected'.

The section entitled 'Walking the Coast', which is in fact one long poem in fifty-three 'bits', came out in a bilingual edition in Paris (Editions du Nouveau Commerce, 1980), under the title *Le Grand Rivage*. A limited art edition, with screen prints by John Christie, had come out from Circle Press (Guildford, Surrey), with the title *A Walk along the Shore*, in 1977.

The section 'North Roads, South Roads' constituted the first part of the book *Mahamudra* which appeared, in a bilingual edition, in Paris (Mercure de France, 1979). I've changed the order, and added several poems written later: 'Remembering Gourgounel', 'In Aquitania', 'Hölderlin in Bordeaux', 'In the Sea and Pine Country', 'Crow Meditation Text', 'Scotia Deserta', as well as some actually written earlier: 'Early Morning Light on Loch Sunart', 'Trail's End', but which all belong essentially

8

here, according to the new sense of itinerary and unity this book carries with it.

Out of Asia was the second part of the *Mahamudra* book. To the poem taken from it I've added 'The Eight Eccentrics' and 'The House of Insight', again written later, but belonging, to my mind at this moment, to that context. Also included in this section are *Scenes of a Floating World*, a sequence which came out first in a bilingual edition in 1976 (Alfred Eibel Editeur, Paris and Lausanne), and was later published, again in a bilingual edition, along with an essay on the 'floating world' and excerpts from 'Chinese notebooks', by the Editions Bernard Grasset, Paris, 1983.

The *Pyrenean Meditations* constituted the first part of the book *Atlantica*, published in Paris (Grasset, 1986). *The Atlantic Movement* made up the second part of that book. To it I've added 'Melville at Arrowhead' and 'First Sketches of the Isles of America'. *The House at the Head of the Tide* was the third part of *Atlantica*. To it I've added 'Broken Ode to White Brittany', which was originally published by William Blake & Co., Bordeaux, in 1980.

I think that more or less completes the story and the map.

'Longer poems' is of course no more than a useful working term. It means, for the sake of something like a sustained tonality, the exclusion here of various types of 'short poem' such as those being gathered into *Handbook for the Diamond Country* which, some day, will be the 'collected shorter poems'.

Kenneth White
North coast of Brittany
August 1988

TABLE OF CONTENTS

THE BIRD PATH

'To tread the bird path' is a Ch'an expression which means realizing the self-nature. A flying bird leaves no tracks in the air, like the self-nature which leaves no traces anywhere, for it is omnipresent and is beyond location and direction.

Note on a remark by Master
Liang Chiai of Tung Shan
mountain, in Lu K'uan
Yü's *Ch'an and Zen Teaching*

You will be a long time on the road, but in Harddlach you will be rejoycing seven white years and the birds of Riannon singing to you over the water.

The Story of Branwen

PROLOGUE

IN PRAISE OF THE ROSY GULL

I.

The ivory gull is beautiful, and one of the toughest birds in the world. Doesn't live in an ivory tower. Unless you call the hell-gates of the Arctic an ivory tower.

Then there's the laughing gull. O, how she laughs. She's a crazy sea-screamer. Nests in the skull of a ghost.

But the rosy gull—there's more to her than a man can say. She has a white head, and breast rose-flushed, and is one of the most secret birds in the world. Few, very few ornithologists have seen her alive.

I love all gulls, but the rosy gull is the one that really possesses me. I see her suddenly now and then, when I speak out largely and clear. I'd like others to see her too. Some people just won't believe that she exists.

They prefer canaries in cages. Or parrots. Or pterodactyls with the whooping cough. I suppose I'm just illiterate.

2.

It was on that shore in the west that I first saw the rosy gull, about fifteen years ago. My sister had told me there was a horse's head just above the waterline to the north of the pier, and I had gone down to see and hide it away among the rocks. I'd wait till the flesh rotted off and retrieve the skull.

I had found the head and was dragging it along the sand when I discovered also this carcass of a seagull. It was unlike any seagull I had ever seen. Its breast feathers were lightly rose-coloured and I thought at first it was blood, but the bird was not wounded, and blood anyway could not cause such beautiful coloration.

For having seen such a strange gull that day, I could not rest till I had at least identified her and found out something of her habits and habitat. This I did by looking up all the bird-books I could lay my hands on.

The results of my investigations were these: this rosy gull is usually considered the most beautiful of all birds in the world. Very little is known about her. In the Arctic winter, when all other birds go south, the rosy gull heads north and winters probably in the very central parts of the Polar Sea, where harsh gales prevail and almost complete darkness . . .

THE COLD WIND OF DAWN

THE BALLAD OF KALI ROAD

a sociocultural extravaganza
for several voices, a tin
whistle, a Jew's harp and a
sense of supernihilism

1.

Coming through the Saltmarket
with the powerful stench of fish in my nostrils
past the pub where the old man's old man
earned a few extra shekels
over the Albert Bridge
and the Clyde's turgid waters
this Saturday morning in October
under a pale blue Indian-summer sky
into what remains of the old South Side:

a few gutted redstone tenements
windows smashed, rubble in the closes—
along the new Crown Street
up to the Gushetfaulds
where Dixon's Blazes, roaring and rumbling
used to cast its lurid glare on the sky
the local image of hell
('if ye don't behave yersel
ye'll get sent tae the Blazes!')
now replaced by a couthy carpet factory
about as inspiring as the *People's Friend*

2.

Don't worry, pal—this won't be a sob-song for *No Mean City*
or a remake of *Miracle in the Gorbals*. The old hell-holes no doubt
had to go. And they're well and truly gone. We'll waste no time
in lamentation. What follows is more in the nature of an
invitation to the dance. A supernihilistic dance on this
cremation-ground the XXth Century has so conveniently
provided for us.

3.

Dancing's always
been in the family
the old man's old man
was a piper and dancer
that is, a Hielant dancer
though he wisnae a teuchter

the old man himself
was hot on the jiggin'
used to shuffle along Florence Street
as one of the Bowler Brigade
used to follow the band
in which his brother played the sax
and would do a bit of singing too
like 'The Birth of the Blues'

but my dance here as you'll gather
is a different kind of thing altogether
having damn all to do
with Highland Reels or 'Stormy Weather'.

4.

I'm what you might call a transcendental Scot.

5.

'Here's tae the good old whisky
drink it down, down, down,
here's tae the good old whisky
drink it down, down, down
here's tae the good old whisky
makes you feel so frisky
here's tae the good old whisky
drink it down, down, down'—
Danny Reilly used to sing that song.

6.

I'm in a pub called Dixon's Blazes
which didn't exist when Dixon's existed
(those were the days of the Hi Hi,
The Rising Sun and 'roon the coarner')
standing all alone in its glory
and cashing in on the old mythology—
because myths won't grow here any more
we're making it on a re-al-ist-ic floor.

7.

Around 1923 in this quarter
my father was collecting rents
for a firm in Bath Street
and was known as 'the wee factor'
but not liking to dun poor folk
he gave up that 'job with a future'
and joined the railway
first on the Carriages and Wagons Staff
then in the signalcabin at Polmadie
where he read Bakunin, Marx, Keir Hardie.

8.

Song about the uselessness of life

We were brought up hale and hearty
though our mother's breast was clarty
and a whisky dribble sometimes touched our lips
we were dragged up by the ears

through a maze of ragged years
and our staff of life was Tally fish and chips

When the nation came to call us
we were fourteen and quite gallus
and we thought the future held the promised land
but the City quickly taught us
that a man's own work and thought is
what the sparrow's to the eagle, to the mighty ocean, sand

We were there to aid production
meant to work without objection
and the prize they held before us was: a wage
just to keep ourselves alive
so the happy few might thrive
and eat the cake of righteousness within their gilded cage

So the slaved enslave the slaves
since we first dwelt in the caves
and Society's a hellish rigmarole
you may think that the Creator
planned it all when on the batter
and may turn your arse sky-blue for the saving of your soul

You may try to get together
call the other man your brother
and the venture may seem hopeful for a spell
you may form associations
you may draw up regulations
but your brother's son will twist them all to hell

About the problem that remains
we have often beat our brains:
is it worthwhile hanging on then after all?
there must be some solution
to society's pollution
if you find it, don't forget to give the call

9.

'Eech harum darum doo
eech harum darum dorus
a think we should aa be shot
for singin' such a rotten chorus!'

10.

A voice from the direction of the Old Wynd Kirk:
'This age also is advancing. Its very unrest, its ceaseless
activity, its discontent contains matter of promise.
Knowledge, education are opening the eyes of the humblest,
are increasing the number of thinking minds ... There is a
deepening struggle in the whole fabric of society; a boundless,
grinding collision of the New with the Old ...'
                    Thomas Carlyle, *Signs of the Times*, 1829

11.

To return to the present.
Cathcart Road, October 11th, 1977

'A waant ma hole
a waant ma hole
a waant ma hole-idays
tae see the cunt
tae see the cunt
tae see the cunt-ery
fu'cu—
fu'cu—
fu'curiosity.'

12.

Western culture's oot the windae
(pattin' peas at its blin' auntie)—
bring on the Dancing Girl!

'Because you love the burning ground
I have made a burning ground of my heart
so that you, Dark One
may enter in and dance
the eternal dance
nothing else is in my heart
o Mother Kali
day and night, night and day
the funeral pyre blazes
and the ashes of the dead
are scattered all around
o Kali
enter in and dance
the rhythmic dance
and I shall watch
with closed eyes.'

13.

The old man's old man as aforesaid
was piper, dancer, and publican
also sodger
of the kind that had lice in their kilts
at Passchendaele and Ypres
his wife was the daughter
of a tea merchant from Inverness
and they all lived together
(there were two boays and two lassies)

at No 439 Crown Street
till Tommy left and got mairit
and Nan left and got mairit
and Ellen left and got mairit
and Willie left and got mairit
to Jennie Cameron, daughter of Baldie Cameron
('Baldie' here being short for Archibald
not indicating lack of thatch)
who toiled in a shirt factory in the Shaws

14.

This hotch-potch might be called: Washing your Dirty Souls in
Public, or Dragging the Ghosts from the Closet, or yet again
Aa Dressed Up an' Naewhere tae Go.

15.

Jock White wound up with a stroke
and lay paralyzed in his bed
till a minister, faith-healer
came to lay hands on him:
'Do you feel the fluid, John,
are you feeling any the better?'
'Oh, aye, Mr Gillespie,
feelin' an awfa lot better'—
like hell:
when the minister was out the door
his son Willie asked the auld buggar
why he'd lied like that—
'Och, a didny waant tae disappoint the man'

a few days later
he gave one last scunnered look
and his troubles were over.

16.

This was Wee Harry Hope's song:

'A went tae the racecourse last July
far far away
the horse a backed was Kidney Pie
far far away
the horse it won a danced wi' glee
a went tae collect ma LSD
where wis the bookie
where wis he
far far away.'

17.

Where is Jock White? Deid.
Where is Danny Reilly? Deid.
Where is Wee Harry Hope? Deid.
Where is Auld Man Graham? Deid.
Where is Nancy Shaw? Deid.
Where is Sarah Tennant? Deid.
Where is Sam the Jew? Deid.
Where is Seek Peter McGee? Deid.
Where is Tam the Busher? Deid.

—deid, deid, deid
aa that's left is ghost stories.

18.

Song of the Coffin Close

Have you heard of the Coffin Close, boys
have you heard of the Coffin Close
it's one of life's rare joys, boys
it smells like a summer rose
yes, it smells like a summer rose

Have you ever climbed up the stair, boys
have you ever climbed up the stair
where the lavvy-pan overflows, boys
and gives you a whiff of rotten air
yes, a whiff of rotten air

Have you ever fallen down the stair, boys
have you ever fallen down the stair
and buried your sensitive nose, boys
in the filth and muck which is there
yes, the filth and muck which is there

Have you ever come up at night, boys
have you ever come up at night
when the burner throws its rays, boys
you see many a ghastly sight
yes, many a ghastly sight

Have you ever seen Bill McNeice, boys
have you ever seen Bill McNeice
lying dead to the world, boys
and a cat being sick in his face
yes, a cat being sick in his face

Have you ever seen Mary Cape, boys
have you ever seen Mary Cape

she often hangs there on the stairs, boys
coughing her insides up
coughing her insides up

You all know the Coffin Close, boys
you all know the Coffin Close
if I bother you all with my noise, boys
it's all for a very good cause
yes, it's all for a very good cause

I live in the Coffin Close, boys
I live in the Coffin Close
very soon they'll be taking me out, boys
and my head will come after my toes
yes, my head will come after my toes.

19.

Ah, well, Kali
let it all go down the river
on the brown waters
under the empty blue sky
let it all
go down the river
down
down the river
to the long shore
the long white shore
where John Knox
is a hermit crab
and Plato
is a jellyfish.

OM SUNYAJNANA KRIM SVAHA
HERE ENDETH THE BALLAD OF KALI ROAD

ZONE

Sun a beetroot thrown in mud
six o'clock winter in Dumbarton Road

oatcakes and milk I buy at the dairy
as cars spit their way towards the ferry

the lampstands caught in beginning frost
send out whiskers of light that are lost

in the electric bonfires of the passing trams
while bored-looking women lug their prams

to family tea. I could go home at once and eat
but I wait till the rush is over in the street

and feel that deep loneliness cover my mind
now the moon has appeared like a turnip rind

above the cranes and the gables. The Caspar Hauser song
trails in my conscience as I trudge along

stopping at the corner to drink the milk
while a cat spick and span in genteel silk

black and with inaccessible eyes surveys with disdain
my enterprise decides he need not remain

and slips off into a close without a backward look
I think I shall make an excursion to Pollok

for I cannot return to my spurious home
where all day I've written of Jonah's tomb

I shall take my trip on the trams and hope
that my spirits will be not too ashamed to elope

with the first image tossed from the city's rusty womb

AT THE SOLSTICE

> *Sur le Noël, morte saison,*
> *que les loups se vivent de vent . . .*
> François Villon

I.

The moon last night was a sheer calamity
a leprous hunchback of a planet
Santa Claus with ice in his sack
had I not gone to bed with the whisky
I'd have surely froze to the floor

as it was, midnight and past
I ascended into the banshee hill
the pipes of winter wildly playing
and the fairy fires of Schiehallion
kindling up my seraphic instinct

they found a lyre in the town of Ur
and its sound-box was a sailing ship
whose figurehead was a bull
two or three millenniums back
this was the instrument I played

I have set my feet in a large room
the nearest thing to the infinite
I am whirling in an orbit of ecstasy
a sudden stirring of matter
and this I call the beginning

2.

The window's like an arctic map
the gutters are choked with wrinkled ice
the sun is a cheese in a fridge
the seat of my pants is as thin as charity
and my backside has a grudge against the world

I go up to the market to feed my poem
the market women have chappit lips
with red and dribbling noses
four layers of wool around their hips
and smiles like a crack in a mirror

the last will and testament of fowls
is throttled at the source
every bird has goose pimples now
even the turkey that tries to coquet
with a tuft of black plumes in its rump

horse flesh is crimson and grim
shrimps are pink and neat in a box
cockles grin with a salt sea-whiteness
mussels keep their red secret close
and oysters writhe in the cold

3.

I stand in my own inscrutable whiteness
and my heart is a blazing furnace
and I try to enlarge my soul
and I know that the deepest is the most alive
and I want nothing less than all

I have grown chrysanthemums in the dung of God
I have blacked my boots with the Bible

and walked all over the world
I have lived in the Chinese mountains
and planted bamboo in drizzling rain

to open your eyes and broaden your chest
and take long easy strides
that is the way
to let the holy ghost breathe mountain air
and eat the wild fruits of the earth

for long the world was an inn
an ale-house back of heaven
where all were benighted and lost
but I say the world is a range of possibles
and the flight of wild poems

4.

Stoke up the fire and light your lamp
never mind the cold and the oncoming dark
take up your books, continue your studies
let no man say you were afraid of the silence
or rotted away in self-pity

animals howl and stare at the moon
take you its force and turn your back
and write in your own whiteness
trace your own progress
all the hidden changes of winter

let the old buzzard snotter and snash
weave the snow to a flannel shirt
with a thick tail to cover your hurdies
use the rain to mix your toddy
and the wind to turn the pages of your book

personal force can work wonders
without it talent is nothing
increase your life
and strengthen your character
make full use of this winter

5.

From Strathclyde to Whiteness lies the way
through all the wild weathers of the world
and through the dog-days: *si con Escos*
qui porte sa çavate, de palestiaus sa chape ramendée
deschaus, nus piés, affublez d'une nate

holding the highway, an upland man
singing loud in the barbary tongue
through the winter to the early spring
no false knowledge in the brain
no contrivance in the heart

the hills are still the same remember
and the rivers and the winds
give yourself room for a real beginning
the man who works in a narrow space
builds no more than prison or grave

I wrote this poem in sixty-two
in December, two days from Christmas
my house is secluded and I live alone
but this is the condition of wandering far
and I know I have companions.

OVID'S REPORT

On the shores of the Black Sea
first century of our era

And they cast me out on the Scythian coast . . .

At first I found it hard to swallow
just imagine, me
Publius Ovidius Naso
one of Rome's brightest lights
well in with Horace and Propertius
a member of the Academy
all alone among uncouth clods
on the cold and foggy banks
of the impossible Black Sea

I spat protest
the stench of swine and seaweed
offended my delicate nostrils
I scratched out elegies
finely wrought discourses
all to no good

In fact, strangely, in time
I found exile to my liking

Divorced from clique and public
with nobody to clap applause
at my capricious wit
I was able
to move off into the dark
and live with it

Between the pigs and the gulls
with no glib talk gliding off my tongue
I was no longer Naso
ad nauseam

the citizenship of Rome
dropped off me
like some old skin
the Midland Sea
suddenly looked wearisome
polluted, overpopulated
its *dolce vita*, insipid
the world opened up
wider and more demanding
than I'd thought

One day
thanks to some frozen river
barbarian hordes
will sweep down over the Latin lands
rushing to meet their future:
civilised primitives
sick of themselves—
I've gone the other way
I've come up North
where I fill my expanded lungs
with a sharper air

Here we are at the world's edge
a land of wind and shadow
on the banks of this rolling obscurity
a place of storm
and hard to navigate:
shallow waters
with short, quick, jabbing
waves
thick fog rising over them
through it at times you'll hear
a wild swan whooping

A long time, long ago
on the docks at Marseilles
in a tavern I met
a sailor from Greece
(Demosthenes was his name)
for a jar or two
he gave me a map—
for years and years
it lay forgotten
but I found it again in my papers
the day I left Rome
since then
it's been my favourite reading

Here's Europe
bound on the South by the Mediterranean
on the West by the Atlantic
on the North by the Sea of Britain
on the East
by the Danube and the Don

We all know Europe (or think we do)
we know Iberia
Celtia, Germania
and the isles of Britannia
we even know Thule
at least, by hearsay
but where we are now
everything's uncertain
all we've got
is a host of questions

Big rivers
moving
through the night of the world:
the quickflowing Ister

that never freezes
the crystal-clear
Borysthenes
and the Tanaïs
wide and calm

This is Scythian land
an erratic, paradoxical people
bold as hell
dying with a laugh on their lips
and mourning the birth of babes
they're tattooed from head to toe
and swill beer
from the skulls of their kin

Up there
towards the sea of ice
roam the Hyperboreans
(unless of course they're just pure myth . . .)
between the Scythians and the Hyperboreans
a hundred people, a thousand tribes
Rome has never heard of:
the Gull Folk
the Star-seekers
the Seal-hunters
the People of the Mist
the Sons of the Wind
the Lonely Ones
the Stone Folk
and so on
ever more and more strange
those who wear shadows
those who fish in emptiness

Beyond the Caspian to the North
a land with no fixed limits

gripped in frost
to the East
the long dusty acres of Asia . . .

Outside the pale
rusticated once and for all
I went (abstractly) native
in art and in love
what I've always been after
and rarely found
was what would take me
the farthest possible out of myself

I've had enough, more than enough
of the all-too-human scene
that stuffy theatre
with its antics and its gestures
all those stories told and told again
what I'm interested in now
are the silent fields
I feel spreading all around me
the movements of the sea
the star-bespattered sky
the relation
between a body and the universe
the nebulae and a brain

I've known storms of the mind
sidereal emotions
intellectual auroras
as if the universe and myself
were one:
I've been
the flight of a crow
I've been
a shower of rain

I've been
black waves breaking in the sky
I've been
an unknown horizon

There's a strange poetry hidden
in the cold streams
of these barbarian lands
the Black Sea isn't black
it's full of unbelievable blues
you won't find Venus there
but fish, yes
and I've seen some queer ones:
like slivers of a dreamworld
meditations in the flesh

On the shores of this Black Sea
wind-blasted, storm-swept
where the flowers
are clinging mosses
reeking weeds
and whorled shells
I've tried my hand again at writing

But with none
of the old decoration
none of that foosty rhetoric
it's a new roughness I'm out for now
a new clearness

I'm no longer
some fancy word-knitter
but the primitive
of a philosophy
whose logic I don't know
whose language I don't speak

I take quick notes
like this:
winter morning light
and a black-winged gull
keening over the hut—
no more than that
no metaphor-mongering
no myth-malarkey

I think of lines
like lightning flashes
lines that in their flying energy
would make things
touch and radiate in the mind

I'll have to be going farther
into this night
get further into
this new space
follow right through
the transhuman road
find, who knows, the source
of another light.

WALKING THE COAST

I

. . . .
              for the question is always
                    how
              out of all the chances and changes
            to select
        the features of real significance
                          so as to make
                  of the welter
                    a world that will last
        and how to order
                    the signs and the symbols
              so they will continue
                  to form new patterns
              developing into
        new harmonic wholes
                  so to keep life alive
        in complexity
                  and complicity
                          with all of being—
        there is only poetry

2

living as a boy on the shore
seeing and hearing
the clou-
ding and clamouring of gulls
like overwhelming metaphors
or maybe a heron
'na h'aonar ri taobh na tuinne
mar thuigse leatha fhèin 's a' chruinne
alone beside the sea
like a mind alone in the universe

3

ah, the gulls:
baagies bluemaws aulins badochs
goos scutiallans
cobbies and *scarts*
colmows collochans fraiks
and scawreys
dungbirds diviegoos goylers merricks
pictarns pickseas
dirtyallans
pleengies redshanks scoultons
swabies
tarrocks and *weathergaws*—
all haphazardly manoeuvring
a hymn to chaoticism
out in the wind
and the lifting waters
and myself there maybe no more
staring from my mind's wide-open door
than *faoileag an droch chladaich*
the gull of a stony shore

4

in that house of three storeys
              only yards from the sea
     a house with
                   anwar don lavar
              levawr wrthi
     a wild wave talking
                   and clashing beside it

                        5

and outside in the darkness
                   the island lighthouse
     a white tower
                   36 feet high
     with the focal plane 90 feet
                        above high water
              showing a white group-flashing light
     with the characteristic
                   of 2 flashes in quick succession
     every 30 seconds
              its effective intensity
     being 200.000 candlepower
                   its range in clear weather
                   16 miles

6

and how it began was
there in the womb of the hills
    seeing that snowhill
                smooring against the sky
        rooted there
                obscure
amazed
                    inarticulate
                            strange
        then a cry

7

goddess
        dark wind blowing in from the sea
                this dawn
    the deep-blue mussel-beds
                    writhe and crackle
            the salt sand
                reflects in its pools
                        the awakened gulls
        and the first
                redness
            as you open your belly
                    over the island
        and the day comes cold and howling

8

like the still warm ashes
of a fire of wood
is the heron's body
now silent at the edge
of its uncouth nest
in the beech's crest
motionless in its swaying heights
and myself there watching
among the red leaves
that litter the earth
winter's torn branches
and
signs of birth
those blue shells
clotted with blood
that smell of the sea

9

Canadian firs
their branches lopped
eyes carved in the bark
eyes
a circle white-yellow
surrounding the dark red
centre wood
resin dripping clear and brown
from the eye-wound
and the sap
turning in the air
to a milky blue—

who in the stillness
gazes here

10

a scurry of red leaves
              and the wind passes over
      rippling the stream
                    the wind is all around
      but only stray gusts enter
             the wood's dark centre
  enter and are gone—
              only scurrying leaves
                    and the rippled stream

11

                              believing
          that the biological
                    aim of art
          is to project around us
  the images
            the proofs
                          the manifestations
      of a power of synthesis
                    at one with life
            and maintaining life
  against solitude
             and fragmentation
          the cold aggressiveness
                    of the space-time world

12

and
that the surface of things
can give enjoyment or disgust
but the inwardness of things
gives life
knowing that the poetry
which says that inwardness
also gives life

13

like
at the turn of the path
in the April wood:
that small world
complex
fortuitous
drenched with brightness
earth
stones
wet grass
and the red
branches of the hawthorn
—outside only the moors
and the bleakness of the glacial drift

14

or like the group of alpine flowers
                    on the heights of Ben Lawers:
                         saxifrage
              mountain pansy
      gentian
                         wood-anemone
          rose-root
                    moss-campion
              angelica
                    dwarf marigold
—a unique assemblage
              due to a series of coincidences
      a small stratum of ideal rock
              well-mineral'd
          not over-acid as in surrounding strata
          on mountains so high
                         that unstable habitats
      have existed there continuously
                    since the post-glacial period
          the plants becoming
                    established in a crack
  their roots breaking up the rock
              by a slow process
      their shoots and leaves
                    collecting rock fragments
          blown by the wind
or washed down by water
              till the soil becomes deeper
and the flowers
          can gather full nourishment
                    and beauty grow

15

the loveliness is everywhere
                    even
          in the ugliest
                    and most hostile environment
          the loveliness is everywhere
                at the turning of a corner
                                    in the eyes
                        and on the lips
                                of a stranger
            in the emptiest areas
                    where is no place for hope
            and only death
                        invites the heart
      the loveliness is there
                        it emerges
              incomprehensible
                          inexplicable
          it rises in its own reality
      and what we must learn is
                          how to receive it
              into ours

16

the pebble of rough
                and unprepossessing stone
            the harsh dull case
                            splits open
        to reveal
                        the lovely agate crystal
                the boulder
                                cut asunder
                        shows
            a blue-gleaming layer of amethyst—
                there is a principle
        of beauty and order
                            at the heart of chaos
                within life there is life

17

it will come again
                    the living thought
            certain as those wings
                            that catch the light
        and exact in its loveliness
                    certain as those wings
                        and
            exact in its loveliness
                            the living thought
        it will come again

18

in the period of spiritual drought
said Kokoschka
the essential values will survive
in spite of all
and then will come the future . . .
I am no defeatist
neither optimist nor pessimist
what I know
is what I see
like a stone falling
like stars gleaming . . .
and why do I squander my life-time painting
because when I am painting
I know myself in the midst
of something living

19

for out of the darkness
                    suddenly
              came the white-haired gulls
              came starlings
                        grotesquely
and thrushes blackies redbreasts
                    noisily
        end of winter movements
              colours movements
                        in my space
    daffodil
        crocus
              primrose
a girl's face
        now what I know
                        must grow
            rain
                    earth

20

living in obscurity
            like Hakuyu
        his name meant
              White Obscurity
        his name meant
              he who lived in the hills
        back of Northern White Water—
or secretly though not unconsciously
        in the cities of Europe
    living my life
                founding and grounding
        a world

21

                    for the higher mind
            is like unto a lump of rosy quartz
                    a curious rock
        whose deep and unified rose-shade
                            is rare in the extreme
            but which even when pale
                                (as when over-heated
                or exposed to strong sunlight
                        it loses its colour)
        can be restored absolutely
                        to its original state
            by complete secretion away for a while
        in a place of darkness
                                wet
                            and cold

22

        the rosy quartz—
                there in loose pieces
            on the beach of Coll
                    in granite belts
        on the north shore of Loch Eatharna
                and in gneiss
            at Poolewe Glen Logan and Rona:
            an image of the soul
                    when it emerges at last
        from the *magma originaria*
                        and through the conflicts—
                an idea of the earth

23

having lived in Germany
                domiciled in Munich
                (soft snow drifting over Schwabing)
in a shack
        where I nearly froze to death
                on the edge of the *Englischer Garten*
                        (thin grassblades held in frost)
        listening at night
                to the blind man's radio
                                howling
                knowing every painting in the *Haus der Kunst*
                        having climbed
                                with my cold barbarian eyes
                every baroque pillar in the city
                                finding no paradise

24

and Munch
        asked about the book he was writing
        the autobiography
                answered
        'I
                have put it aside
                it is
        nothing but chaos
                        nothing
                                but
                                        chaos'
        and
        'I am very lonely here' he said
                'but I go on
                                working quietly'

25

it was of Goethe
            that Groddeck wrote:
' He understood
the great secret
    and tried
        to live his life
                in accordance with it
                    merging his separate existence
            in the life of nature
and this is the reason
            why we feel him
        so strange and yet familiar
        so cold and remote
    yet brimming over with energy
            and life-determination'

26

in Paris also
            where
from my little window
    on the 7th floor
I could see the red light
    on the Eiffel Tower
pointing the obscurity
        I breathed in

27

having lived in Glasgow
            lodged in a large dark room
with three shelves of books
            a table a chair a bed
on the floor a rough carpet
(Connemara red)
            in one corner a rug
(a goatskin from Tibet)
on the first wall was pinned
            a print of Hokusai
on the second was
                        an X-ray photo of my ribs
on the third was
            a long quotation from Nietzsche
on the fourth was
                        nothing at all
            that's the wall I went through
            before I arrived here

28

knowing now
that the life
at which I aim
is a circumference
continually expanding
through sympathy and
understanding
rather than an exclusive centre
of pure self-feeling
the whole I seek
is centre plus circumference
and now the struggle at the centre is over
the circumference
beckons from everywhere

29

for
like Kandinsky
returning to his studio at twilight
and seeing a canvas
'of indescribable
and incandescent beauty'
it happens
that the 'known' materials of my life
sunk almost into oblivion
by familiarity
suddenly blaze out
materia poetica
of new realities
each time more complex
and I advance

30

so that when a physicist
                    far out in his field
          says the starting-point
                for the realm of unknowns
                    is a
'universe of contrasts
                    grouped into
          complexes of relations
      with aspects of
                    order and disorder
                including
                    change and tendency'
I say that's it
        that's my territory
      that's the world I'm living through
                    and trying to work out

31

and when a Japanese literatus
            speaks of the series of *waka* poems
      (sometimes as many as 100 in a sequence)
                    written in the Kamakura period
                        (13th and 14th centuries)
          saying 'the result
                was often a kind of kaleidoscopic beauty
                            with infinite variety
          revealed to the reader
                in a slowly evolving movement'
I recognize my aim

32

even crystals
        know disorder and shadow
     but since our aim is not perfection
          but natural form
               in movement
      this will not deter us
        or cause us
    to plunge ourselves into
        morbid disintegration
   we must think in reality clearly
     knowing that
given a sufficiently
    complex ground of signs
       even the most acute
of the problems of disorder
          may be solved
    through what is called
        semi-classical approximation

33

'Who, if I cried
                would hear me
        from the ranks of angels
            and even if suddenly one
                should take me to his heart
I would perish of his stronger presence
for the Beautiful is nothing
                but the onset of the Terrible
            still just endurable
        and we admire it so
                    that serenely
        disdains to destroy us
                every angel is terrible
    so I hold myself in check and swallow
            the darkly-sobbing call
    alas whom then can we use
        not angels not men
and the cunning animals
        have noticed already
    that we are none too securely
            at home
            in the interpreted world'

34

let us speak no more of angels
but of the Great Skua
skimming down
the east coast of Scotland
with stercorant gab
in a windy and white september
or of the Grey Heron
flustering to rest
with outstretched shanks
and a fraiking throat
after lonely fishing
on the Ayrshire coast
on a darkblue august evening

35

for the moment now
is as the one marked so
on the barometer
set in the wall
at North Street
in the town of St Andrews
(a redness on the water
this April morning
low grund and sharring of the waves
against the pier)—
'when rise begins
after low squalls
expect clear blow'

36

now here in the north
                beyond the barren red
        in the outbrecks
    ortan in this husky weather
                at my owdny of a poem
        living out on this grand
                    that runs into the sea
        with fanns of whiteness
            drifting up against my windows
writing in goliment
            till I get da whole fargis
        on to da page
                    tinks du I'll make it
            by God I will try

37

in this house
            where the wood on the stone
                    burns brightly red
        this house
            where the candle
        glows with a lithe
                    blue-hearted flame
                    this house
        where the girl's gull-body
                    lies in her nakedness
            and the high north wind
        has been blowing now
                for ten white days

38

there's only one man here
     to keep me company
   and that's Thomas of Cromarty
     his ghost
    who is a walking gramary
 and *Altus Prosator* in person
     craggy and crazy
   like a crop of lewisian gneiss
    overlooking the coast
with seven types . . . of lightning
     flickering round its crest
    and
deep in the heart of its darkness
    belly-laughing chaos

39

Urquhart
        inherits a 'crazed estate'
                in the extreme north of Scotland
    sets himself up a library
                (later confiscated by usurers)
        with books gathered from sixteen countries
                        in the mansion of Cromarty
            and writes
                a pedantic and fantastic
                        treatise on trigonometry
                    called *Trissotetras*
                a *Pantoxponoxanon*
                            to deduce the genealogy
of the Urquharts
                from the red earth in the hands of God
        a translation of Rabelais'
                Gargantua and *Pantagruel*
        and *Logopandecteision*
                an introduction
    to the possibilities
            of framing 'a new idiome
            of far greater perfection'
        than all existent languages
    for all
        'pregnant and ingenious spirits'
                dying
                at the age of about sixty
                    suddenly
on the continent
        in a fit of excessive laughter

40

though I think too at times
        of Donnacha ban nan Orain
    whose wife
            was a dandy whisky distiller—
and of Alasdair MacMhaigstir Alasdair
        the man who wrote the *birlinn*—
                and of Iain MacCodrum nan Ron
        who wrote the rabelaisian
                        Oran na Muice
        and who chose an enormous and amorphous
    lump of gneiss
                for his gravestone—
and of Hugh MacDiarmid
            composing the caledonian wake
        circumveiloped in obscuritads
                and
ortan like an ox in an ootdyke

41

and *larus atricilla*
                              Laughing Gull
        pagophila eburnea
                              Ivory Gull
    rhodostethia rosea
                              Rosy Gull
            these also
                          are here in the darkness
                totems gleaming in the night
                              like *adee*
            the Kwakiutl thunderbird
                    up there
        in the High Northwest of America
            for this is my potlatch poem
(since
            as father Rabelais says
                '*heureux nous resputons*
                              si à autruy
tousjours donnons
                          et eslargissons beaucoup')
            being one of those
                '*beaulx livres*
                          de haulte graisse'
            that must come out of this time
                      for survival
        so Indians Chinese and Eskimos
                  scientists and fellow-poets
        all souls of our delirious earth
                  grant me help
            come succour my brain
                I am saying my prayers
    for the first time in years
                    I need everything

42

having no matter where I be
                        a studio in the wood
        as in this Chinese painting now before me
                ground of tree rock earth grass
                cut by precipitous waters
                        painted by the monk Shang-jui
        1729
                in the style of T'ang Yin
                        one of the Four Great Masters

43

                living and writing at random
        but knowing
                that
though living at random
                        there is a tendency to stress
                the essential in the random

44

following the path
that 'path compendious
deviating from common obliquity'
which Michael Scot
the leading mind in western Europe
in the early 13th century
an *'internationalgebildeter Mann'*
with a mass of knowledge
crystallising in his brain
into shining thought
and a love of complexity
that makes him delight
in distinguishing say
sidus from *astrum* and
both from *stella*
and all three from
signum imago or *planeta*
(repugnant to content himself
with a numb generic)
calls
'the way of true science
which is poetry's commencement'

45

the poem being
                    what happens when
          a welter of substantial
                              feelings and facts
have passed through the thalamus
                    the belly of the brain
          and ascended
                    without short-circuiting
          right up into the cortical region
                from where
                          abstracted
            they return again
                          worded on the tongue

46

        elsewise
                    an attempt
              to get at and say out
                    all
      that the world comprises
                    which man
              only rarely
                          realises

47

or again
like the lightning that leaps
from the percussion of stones
like the
thin blue ripple of light
made by the swing of an axe in the air
like the easy
climb and curve of a wave
and its free fall into foam

48

and finally
a complex symbol
placing the accent
on the union of contraries
stressing
the one in the many
the possible
difficult harmony
in the human conscience
the ἁρμονια of Heraclitus

49

but always
                 exemplary language
       subtle as flowers
            plastic as waves
flexible as twigs
                 powerful as wind
         concentred as rock
    syncratic
           as the self
       beautiful as love

50

some like the girasol
       turn their blossom to the sun
     some bloom only in the dark
          like the cereus
       that waits on midnight
or the convolvulus
         that unfolds
     its moonlike petals
          with the setting sun
     perhaps the simplicity
of the wood anemone
        its serenity
       its direct access
   to the energy of the sun
         and the richness of the earth
     might have evolved
        a quieter fuller brain
than the hurry-scurry of animal existence
     on which we have depended

51

who has not observed it
            the primal movement
      the play of wind on water
                        the undulation
            the glassy membrane
      lifted
                  excited
                        and energised
            by insisting air
                  the curving
                        the deliberate inflection
      the flurry of whiteness
                  the bright cast of spray
the long falling rush
                  and the hundredfold ripple

52

even if we had only
    those few scattered rocks on the shore
            (the wind tonight
  blowing hard with rain over the sea)
         how much
   there would be to be learned
       for it is possible
    to live with the rocks
           in unity of mind
and perhaps one who knows
          even one rock thoroughly
  in all its idiosyncracy
        and relatedness
    to sea and sky
  is better fit to speak
        to another human being
than one who lives and rots perpetually
      in a crowded society
    that teaches him
          nothing essential

53

like this rock now before me
      facing the tide
  an outcrop
    of dark grey sandstone
       (so the ones on which
        as children
we chiselled our signs)
    with a blaze
      of white granite
running right through it—

      understand this, poet

NORTH ROADS,
SOUTH ROADS

THE BIRD PATH

1. *Of Childhood*

Raised on stilts
above the tide-line
the boats stood
like eyeless birds
bodies encrusted
with salt and shells

2. *Of the City*

Once I lived in that city:

haar on my window
a crazy light

men with red dreams
in dark corners

a girl brought
the evangel of sex

I studied
the language of dawn

3. *Of Studies*

It was Bhartrihari who said
that grammar leads to beatitude

I've cut the pages, hold it in my hand
open it, and see the black script stand

like the marks a drunken gannet
might leave on the sand

4. *Of the Territory*

Up here in the white country

any tree for a totem
any rock for an altar

discover!

this ground is suicidal

annihilates everything
but the most essential

poet—your kingdom

5. *Of the Emptiness*

This is the cold island

lying on the bare stones
gulls crying in the mist—

the immensity of nothing
empties the veins and bones

6. *Of the Way South*

Among the dark sand
and the rosy seaweed

the deep-curved
sea-white clam shell—

she is scattered
over all the earth

7. Of the Pine Country

Pinetrees
slender-trunked pinetrees
slender dark-tufted pinetrees
slender dark-tufted rain-glistening pinetrees

resin
dripping slowly
from their rosy slits

INTERPRETATIONS OF A TWISTED PINE

> *Learn of the pine from the pine*
> Matsuo Bashô

1.

I started off
by growing up
like everybody else

2.

Then I took

a bend to the south
an inclination east
a prolongation north
and a sharp turn west

3.

Now, approaching me
be prepared for grotesquerie

there are more than pines in my philosophy

4.

Yes I'm something more than a pine
I'm a cosmological sign

5.

I'm idiomatic
I'm idiosyncratic

I'm pre-socratic

6.

I'm maybe Chinese too

like Li Po, Tu Fu
and Mr Chuang-tzu

7.

I live quietly
but storms visit me

I do a metaphysical dance
at the heart of existence

8.

The branches of my brain
are alive to sun and rain

my forest mind
is in time with the wind

there is reason in my resin

9.

Behold the mad pine
stark on the sky-line

HAIKU OF THE SUD-EXPRESS

*With regard to a unity in life, art and
mental attitude, there is no other artist for whom
it is so harmonised as for the haiku poet.*
Santei

1.

North-South, East-West
this man's identity
is difficult

2.

Watching the frost-world
while my two fellow travellers
talk about management

3.

Thinking of my old room:
the cup with the broken handle
that became a bowl

4.

Farther back still:
white sun shining
on the stones of the moor

5.

A railway-cabin flashes by
I hear my father
whistling in the silence

6.

Running around
in crazy circles
a young dog in the snow

7.

Three cities
would take several tellings
I laugh to myself

8.

Midday or thereabouts
I eat my rough biscuits
with a lot of saliva

9.

Field after field
my eyes can't see
enough of this whiteness

10.

Sun reflected
in ice over running water
this joyless joy

11.

Snow drifting
this man's identity
is very simple

REMEMBERING GOURGOUNEL

Ardèche, early sixties

Abandoned house, abandoned soil
walls tangled in thorns and vines
who'd waste energy on land like this
could work it years and no return
but here's a stranger, God knows why
pitching in to clear the rubble and ruck
sweat trickling down his brow and back

Old mulberries that still bear leaves
though some are on their last legs
gutted out and all out of shape
hanging on crazily to the sunburned slope
bees nesting in them, honey gathers
leave 'em where they are then, even the wrecks
they're still in touch with spinning girls

Hacking out a path among the whin
metal of mattock sparking rock
hot flies buzzing around my sweat
blue mist far away down the valley
sun throbbing fiercely in empty sky
a hawk circles quietly over the wood
snake slithers into matted grass

Goat's cheese from the neighbouring stead
and apricots fresh from this morning's tree
with rose-coloured wine from a trappist cell—
I lie still here among thorn and bramble
cool in the shadow at my midday meal
watching blue smoke rising from the western hill
and white cloud sailing over Thunder Mountain

The smith has wrought me a handy axe
just the length I need for swinging
now up in the dark wood cutting rafters
clean axe-head neatly lopping branches
then piling together tumbled stones
will have to learn how to build up walls
make a good job of that old tower

Work over, down to the hillside stream
clear water splashing by the little fall
wash myself enjoying the water's feel
seeing the dragonflies skimming the pool
darkblue-winged in the evening glow
and butterflies like fluttering petals
all the colours of the rainbow

Long hours at night beside the lamp
studying the ten books gathered here
stars clustered thick at the little window
wind soughing coolly in the chestnut wood
a rat scuttles overhead in search of grain
my eyes settle down on the page again
that bird cry is the early dawn.

IN AQUITANIA

Prologue

I'll show you the tombstone, he said
no, not the tombstone, the . . .

'Flamen and duumvir
questor and district chief
Verus
having acquitted himself in Augustus' presence
of the charge that had been laid upon him
obtained for the nine peoples
their separation from the Gauls—
back home from Rome
he dedicates this altar
to the genius of the place'

1.

Wind blows down from the meseta
warm rain drifts in from the ocean

fir-trees brush the snow-line
high hill beeches
hold coldness in their foliage
heather and tough grass grip the sandy edge

on flakes of sandstone
on pebbles, on fragments of bone
they draw birds and deer
and hares and horses
salmon and seals

maybe somebody
wandering in the hills
raises that horse-cry
that starts down guttural low
and winds up whinneying high

2.

After the ice, the sea rises
rivers swollen
low valleys flooded
all along the littoral
lagoons and marshes

the coast seeping with wetness

dripping caves

people perched
on the hills and ridges

keeping watch

3.

Basque azilian
lasts into the atlantic phase

Maluquer speaks of a
*'vida neolítica
con una economía de recolectores'*

the face of the coast
wrapped in mist

maybe down to the shore
in winter
(red deer went down then
to feed on seaweed and
coastal grass)

a diet of deermeat and shellfish
acorns and hazelnuts

4.

Clearing forests by burning

marsh dwellings

early words for
weaving
tilling the soil
the same as in Caucasian

(old stories:
the pagans grew wheat
at the mouth of their caves)

sub-boreal, sub-atlantic

on to sheep, cattle, goats and pigs

5.

As the Basco said:
'In the Pyrenees my father keep sheep
his father keep sheep
his father . . .'

those black-headed sheep
with the curling horns
that have moved
from winter to summer
between the valley
and the mountain pasture

from time immemorial

'deep are the trails
on these vales and hills'

6.

Maybe at the beginning
the whole tribe moved
in a nomad way
then some went, some stayed:
transhumance

big stone burials
(and shelters?)

dolmens
along tracks, ridges
watersheds, crests

open views to the east

cromlechs higher up
windy peaks

rites (of different types?)

Eastwards
to catch the dawning sun
and give protection
from the westerlies

7.

Real writing had deserted Rome
(Virgil and Ovid long gone)
it went on
in the Greek-minded cities of Provence
or, in a quieter way
here in Aquitania
where the stone world
still spoke to the ocean
and mind was open to wind:

Ausonius to Theon:
'you who plough
the sandy lands of the Atlantic'

and to Paulus:
'where the swollen waters
of the Garunna
provoke the sea'

8.

The rhythm continued

men were there
to see to things
and draw the lines

the landscape grew

it was possible
to speak of peopled place
and cultured space

'quiet Aquitania
on the verge of Ocean'

brought forth from work
and from meditation

9.

This morning at Grayon
I dedicate this inadequate poem
to the dune carnation

the dune carnation
little pink flower
its last home here
on these Aquitaine sands

little pink flower
carrying the whole of history
in its slender roots

a world in miniature
and religion, of a sort

destroyed
by fools on motor-bikes
in the name of sport

HÖLDERLIN IN BORDEAUX

Not overgiven to conversation
when opinions
began trotting off the tongues
he tended to go away
for a walk along the river

'Why be a poet in such wretched times? . . .
I do what I can as well as I can . . .
it all belongs
to the work in hand . . .'

That was in the red days of Autumn
with the grapes ripened
on the Garonne hills
and the memories of friends
who had left on ship
from the windy promontory . . .

Back in Germany
they had nothing for him
but he would go back
back
back to what?
some window overlooking a forest maybe
a little philosophical light . . .

Every day boats left the harbour
for the Indies, the Americas
he paced the quais
and watched them leaving
his journey
lying in another direction—
but how far would he be able to go
when everything was overgrown
with habit and with triviality
and mere opinion?

One may think of Greece
translate the tragedies
indulge in that archaic hyperbole
dream the ideal
the landscape had changed
utterly changed
he'd felt it crossing Auvergne
that awful night
losing his way
in the ice and snow
he'd felt it
the landscape had changed
colder
craggier
more massive—
poetry itself would have to change

No gods to sing to
in a sun-filled theatre
a nothingness to face
in an open expanse . . .

Walking the streets of Bordeaux
in the red days of September
watching how the shadows
moved slowly with the sun
seeing at some high window
a beautiful face
that was there, then gone

He would have to learn
how to travel alone.

CAPE BRETON UPLIGHT

Prolegomena

*Just off Cape Breton, the sea, which elsewhere round the shores of Britain
and France remains at the level of the continental plateau, plunges directly
to oceanic depths of 5,000 metres and more, once inhabited by some of
'the big fish God created': blue whale, finn whale, goose-beaked whale
. . . On these grounds, the area seemed a good place to settle in and work
with for a while. Always the search for the place and the formula, the
essential locality and the few necessary words.*

1.

Is there
        anywhere on the dwindling earth
a man like me
        walking at the edge of the sea
        and

2.

Blue shingle
                 smooth pebble
        dune-grass
           express only the essential
     fix the mind

3.

White-blow of the waves
           confused beginnings
       dissolution and amplitude
               the emptiness is plenitude
     and the gulls
         raise their spontaneous cries

4.

Osprey
            gannet
       white-arsed petrel
   pelagians and hyperboreans
      tantric gulls
    on this ascetic shore
         the abandoned ground
     we haunt

5.

Inland
          the lack of reality
      the reduction of spirit
               is ugly and wearisome
        the mind rots
             language decays
under cypher and strident opinion
            raised up as reason
       the earth disappears
              from the minds of the living
      the real word is lost

6.

At the edge of the world
         in the emptiness
      maintaining the relations
        the primordial contact
            the principles by which
     reality is formed
         on the verge of the abstract

7.

And always the question
      is of unifying
     simplifying
        penetrating

8.

Are the waters female?
        or is woman a coastline
    moulded by the wind?
                walk here girl
    where everything
            answers your nakedness
        eye and sex
                washed in these elements
            and the cry of your body
at one with the cry of the gulls

9.

This morning
        the coast is transparent
    and the highest reaches
                of the mind
    are in their element

10.

The violence of poetry
        is still
                and goes deep—
    to the bone
        to the white

II.

Many images blur the mind
    the highest poetry
        is stricken
     with poverty of image
   when the white light
       gleams at its blindingest
  all objects disappear
      the skull like a sun

THE REGION OF IDENTITY

Before all my arrogant poems, the real
Me stands yet untouch'd, untold,
altogether unreach'd.
       Whitman

It was evening when I got to that beach, after a couple of
hundred miles hitching—the time to find a suitable place to lay
out my sleeping-bag (in the lee of a drifted, sea-bleached
treetrunk), and just to sit there listening to the tide and watching
the stars come out, till I turned in. During the night there was a
storm, a theatre of amber and blue electricity away down the
horizon, with rain coming across the sea in squalls. When I
woke, the sky was miraculously clear, and I had that whole
coast, ten or twelve miles of it unbroken, all to myself. I started
walking . . .

1.

How many forms discarded
      how many selves destroyed
     how many dawns and darknesses
    until I reach
        this place of light and emptiness
   where white birds cry
       a presence—
     or still yet only sign?

2.

So much life lived
      for this one flame
  so much travelling
     for this one point—
 the intelligence trembles
         at the silent approach
        of naked being

3.

The hard path of the spirit
     leads to these places
  all powerful feeling
      leads to these emptinesses
   the destiny of words
     to these moving silences

4.

Or still yet only sign?—
                to cover my naked body
            with signs
            and be a sign among signs
        or to go beyond signs
                into the light
                        that is not the sun
                    into the waters
                            that are not the sea

5.

Always the metaphysical landscape
                but more and more abstract
            yet more abrupt
                    where the farthest of unrealities
            are the reality
        and life
                that dancing flurry
    that line of white
                that incandescent edge
                        advancing
                    beyond meaning and problem

6.

Metaphysical?
                —the physical absolute
            the opaque burned out
                    the heaviness dissolved

7.

This pool of water
                    holding rock and sky
          traversed by the wing-flash of birds
                         is more my original face
             than even the face of Buddha

8.

Panic colony:
                    arch-traces on the sand
          flying whiteness in the air
                         the principles are here—
                                   my species

9.

Cosmic body
                    the cosmo-comedy

THE BHODI NOTEBOOK

in the southern Spring

1.

Little japanee apple-tree
saying quietly:
no need to go to Kyoto

2.

Over the grasses
two white butterflies
fluttering by whitely

3.

Old Hakuin
listening to the snow
out there at Shinoda

4.

What's that? What's that?
the moon
reflected in my soup

5.

Dark, dark
a sudden flash of light
illuminates the yellow whin

6.

Young mountain peak
take off that shirt of mist
so I can see your snowy nakedness

7.

Me and my silence
drinking tea together—
how are things, boy?

8.

Another presence
in the empty room—
ah! the rain

9.

All those teachings—
the summit, OK
the rest, my own way

IN THE SEA AND PINE COUNTRY

1.

Meditation isn't mummification
it's quick movement
that enlightens the mind
those waves
crossing and intercrossing
rising and breaking
here in this dawn
that
is the perfect *zazen*

2.

Here
on the white beach
with nothing in my rucksack
but an empty notebook:
'OK, we know you've studied
but what have you SEEN?'
—Shoji to Hakuin—
waiting and watching

3.

Thinking of another shore
—no, not *the* Other Shore—
I keep going back
to that local shore
a thousand miles away
and what I see there
is nothing marvellous or pure
I see myself pitching
a basin of wormy old meat
from the butcher's shop
into the tide
and the gulls swooping down
in a fierce ragged
wing-flapping flurry
for the feed

4.

Slap slap of the tide
I must be about eight years old
sitting on a rock
it's raining
a grey wet world
watching the tide come in
swirling round the rock . . .

5.

There are no rocks here
only long miles
of absolute sand
with pools that mirror
the summer sky
a flock of gulls
over yonder
flutters into movement now and then
and an occasional cry
enlarges the silence

6.

Long silence, long joyance

7.

At midday
I go into the woods
from the shining sands
to the dark bed of pine:
whin-bushes yellow
crimson gashes on the tree-trunks
sharp smell of resin

8.

'Learn of the pine
from the pine'

9.

Quiet
the wind has dropped
now it is a question
of looking and smelling:
crimson gash, yellow flower
take them
and set the mind on fire

10.

Let the light come
so you can say
really seeing them:

crimson gash, yellow flower
(seeing and saying
then
is power)

11.

Change of scene:
dark sea
the red circle of the sun

12.

Tonight I shall sleep in the woods

CROW MEDITATION TEXT

Everybody knows
the sad sweet tale
of the nightingale
but when crow starts croaking
hard and hoarse
that's something else

crow, I tell you, is one queer joe

crow is a ghost
he's a bird with a past

crow is king
of his own mad world
in which he's always croaking

usually
nobody listens to crow

but when one of your friends
takes off for the icelands
and writes back in a letter
about a weird crow-encounter
somewhere in the snowfields
and when a few days later
as you come through the door
of a Montparnasse apartment
the first thing you set eyes on
is a huge lump of a crow
whose croaking days are over
but looks as if it knew
a thing or two

you begin to wonder
you find yourself asking
what there is to crow

why does crow crow?
where does crow go?
what does crow know?

crow first of all
is polyglottal

crow talks double dutch
with a mixture of eskimo
russki, nahuatl
sanskrit, chinese, snohomish
as well as several brands of english

crow has been around!

Edgar Allan Poe
was a crow

the anthropologist *enyerbado*
turned into a crow

I suppose all the Crows
were crows

I once thought of founding
an Academy of Gulls
(based on an ancient
Chinese model)
with one aim in view:
say the world anew
dawn-talk
grammar of rain, tree, stone
blood and bone

I can conceive of black gulls
and white crows
(no race fiends need apply)
I mean crow could also be
of the Gull Academy
the croaking member

but that plan went with the wind
and I ended up
with broken wings
on a cold island

smoking the weeds of my mind

anyway
the fact is
bird-men are still going around
thinking a feathered dream
croaking, yelling, squawking
all relative heavyweights
which is to say
no warbling or chirping

it's a tough world
and you have to be able
to go it through blizzards

ka, kaya-gaya, ka
krr, krarak, krarak
krie, krie, krie

drink cold water
feed on stones and bones
keep cool and fit

far out on your own

engaged
in long-distance communication

why does crow crow?
where does crow go?
what does crow know?

ask hawk
hovering up there in silence

ask the snowy owl

ask the great skua
and the rosy gull

all birds
talk dawn-talk
in different lingos

POEM TO MY COAT

—a grotesquerie—

> *My coat's all worn after so many years*
> *shreds of it are blowing in the wind*
>   Bokuju

1.

Rain, earth and salt
have worked themselves into the cloth

the perfumes of girls
the stench of cities

old coat,
with the familiar stink of life

let us go on another journey

2.

Let us penetrate once again
the pelagian country

the body of our early love

happy to walk the rocks
and to move among gulls

through an easy ecstasy

heading northwards
in the arctic light

3.

And the wind comes to meet us
the cold wind of dawn

with a bible in one hand
a lump of quartz in the other

and a gull on his shoulder

greeting us like a brother
who's been away in foreign parts

more difficult areas

welcoming us in gaelic
(the three phrases he remembers)

and refreshing us
with a little rain distilled

by his sister the west

4.

Walking along the shore
remembering the past

grasping it in several ways
the better to know it

and penetrate beyond appearances
into the secret nerve:

pelagian orgies
pushed to the limit!

5.

Old shamanskin, listen
while we're moving farther on

this poem is for you
I'll pin it on your lining

may we remain long together
through all kinds of weather

and enjoy the travelling

CRYPTOLOGY OF BIRDS

In form like a bird it appears
(Chippewa medecine-lodge song)

1. *Sula bassana*

Old whitehead philosopher
with a fishy beak
and a crazy eye

the way you squawk
means more than all the talk

2. *Fulmaris glacialis*

The cool path of your flight
puts a silence in the world

buddha of the ice

3. *Larus canus*

Common as hell
the evangel bird

watch it on any shore
writing on air, sand and water

4. *Hydrobates pelagius*

That's a mere sign:

but the stormy petrel
is a violent act of flesh
a wing-beat
from horizon to horizon

disclosing being

5. *Larus ridibundus*

Beyond the immobile silence
hah!

that laugh in the air

THE GANNET PHILOSOPHY

*Every time I go down to the shore, I see it: an ancient gannet, ugly as Socrates
and with a very chilly eye, wings firm in the wind.*

*It was this grotesque angel that, years ago, led me away from
frequented paths and roads—into a great emptiness, where the wind is
shamanistic, and cold bites the bone.*

Up in that white world, existence seemed difficult, if not impossible—till, gradually, I became acclimatised, naturalised, recognising that others had known these regions before me, and that there was even a culture, however scattered, however obscure, attached to them, growing from them.

An extreme culture, full of a hard beauty that had never run to waste, firmly grounded and yet winged.

When Nietzsche cries: 'Let every body become a dancer and every spirit a bird,' he is calling for white world culture. And when the Zen master says: 'The place of the spirit is nowhere, it's like the tracks of birds in the sky,' he is referring to the white world, and of the way to it, which is the bird-path . . .

1.

Way up north
where the great wind blows
he is walking

way up north
where the dawn-light breaks
he is walking

way up north
in the difficult land
he is walking

2.

The more I walk
this northern coast

the closer I am to the East

though I bear the soil of Europe
in my bones

it is an Eastern light I see
striking these stones

3.

The white hills
have perfect reflections:

I came through Lochaber
in the dead of winter

to meet Matsuo Bashô
on the Island of Dogs

4.

All poetry comes
from facing a loveliness

all love comes
from living in nakedness

all naked life
comes from the nothingness

5.

Let your poem
be as the gannet's wing

with power and clarity
in its wheeling

bearing erotic flesh
to the ecstasy of being

LETTER FROM HARRIS

> *Although I compose poetry, I do not*
> *think of it as composed poetry.*
> Saigyo

1.

The degree of isolation
is higher here
than in most places

2.

'The ancient foreland
is continued
in the islands of the Outer Hebrides
which mainly consist
of lewisian gneiss
a metamorphic rock
over 200 million years old

These islands
stretch for a distance
of some 150 miles
along the west coast of Scotland
and are exposed
to the full force
of the Atlantic waves and weather.'

3.

Rodel
where the young men
built the beautiful ship
that the sea coveted
and the 'great cleric' lived
who founded the grammar school in Paris
Rodel this evening
is an empty harbour
a rusty iron ring
and a heap of red seaweed

4.

I asked the old woman
if she liked it here
she answered:
'I'm here whether I like it or not'
and asked about the life she said:
'£1.50 a score of herring
£40 a ton of coal
14p a loaf of bread.'

5.

I open the book
and the words
fly out of the page:
faoileann

   annlag mhara
  bòdhag
    breac-an-t-sìl
—as I listen to them talking
the remaining ones
I hear their phrases
twining and intertwining
like carving on a stony crypt
or like the glorified lines
of a precious manuscript . . .

6.

But when I walk alone
the rocks or the machair
the silence itself is illuminate
and I do not think of culture
or even of subsistence
the question in my mind
is of going outward
always farther outward
to the farthest *line of light*

7.

Phone re boat.
Mr Nicholson. Grimsay 08-2380.
Millar Mundie. 2 Floddabay. 83-234.

'Calum Iain McCorquodale
might be able to take you
but I cannot
give you his phone number
I believe he has the phone now
but his number
is not yet in the book
anyway
you go and see him
and if he's going out
he'll take you
and if he's not going out
too bad.'

Ronald MacDonald of Pabblesgarry.
Angus Cunningham, *The Sapphire*.

8.

The thousand shimmerings
this morning the sea of the monks
is a thousand shimmerings

9.

'We think
of these northern islands
as storm-bound and mist-wrapped
yet nowhere
can there be greater
brilliance of colour
the sea so blue
the rocks so vivid
with saffron lichen

A meadow of sea pink
in June
contains all colours
between white and deep purple
and the white-feathered birds
reflect the boreal intensity
of the summer light'

10.

Medusae
on the white sand beach:
colour of brandy and whisky
or again
infinitely pale—
like the first clutch of living jelly
in a darwinian dawn

11.

'The disciple
sits for long hours
silent and motionless

till he enters
a state of impassivity
free of all thoughts

finally departing from the self
he penetrates
the domain of emptiness.'

12.

A guillemot
reflected
in the glassy water

shatters its image

13.

In the room of roaring waves

EARLY MORNING LIGHT ON LOCH SUNART

1.

While I write this
a grey heron
is standing motionless
in the early morning light
of Loch Sunart

2.

At the centre
of a ring of silence
a grey heron
only the waters rippling
(language dare not be loud this morning)

3.

For still words (long fallen silent)
listen (if you will) to these:
gheibte bradan fioruisg ann
a' dìreadh ris gach sruth
eòin an t'-sléibh gu lìonmhor

4.

A grey heron
watching, listening
in an early morning
glitter of waters—
maybe dreaming?

5.

Fishing in nothingness
(that is one way of putting it)
here on Loch Sunart
bright falling of the year
quiet, so quiet

SCOTIA DESERTA

All those kyles, lochs and sounds . . .

*

And the gulls at Largs pier:
sitting in that café
at the big window full of wind and light
reading and watching

Thinking back to the ice
watching it move
from the high middle spine
out into the Atlantic

feeling it gouge out lochs
and sculpt craggy pinnacles
and smoothe long beaches

the land emerges
bruised and dazed
in the arctic light

gannets gather on the islands
eagles on the piney hills
cotton grass tosses in the wind

men come
gazing around them
what name shall be given it?
Alba

*

White beach meditations
mountain contemplations
imprinted on the mind

*

One left traces of his presence
out there in Bute and the Garvellach Isles
and in Kilbrannan Sound—
the holy voyager, Brandan

Brandan was maybe a believer
but that's neither here nor there
first and foremost
he was a navigator
a figure moving mile by mile
along the headlands
among the islands
tracing a way
between foam and cloud
with an eye to outlines:

Sound of Islay
the Firth of Lorn
Tiree passage
the Sound of Mull
Skerryvore and Barra Head
Loch Alsh, Kyle Rhea
Sound of Raasay

Ah, the clear-sounding words
and a world
opening, opening!

*

Other figures cross the scene
like this one:
Kentigern they cried him

in the church I attended
around the age of nine
was that stained glass window
showing a man

with a book in his hand
standing on a seashore
preaching to the gulls

I'd be gazing at the window
and forgetting the sermon
(all about good and evil
with a lot of mangled metaphor
and heavy comparison)
eager to get back out
on to the naked shore
there to walk for hours on end
with a book sometimes in my hand
but never a thought of preaching in my mind

trying to grasp at something
that wanted no godly name
something that took the form
of blue waves and grey rock
and that tasted of salt

                         *

A rocky walk
and the smell of kelp
between Fairlie and Largs

Drifting smoke
the glint of autumn leaves
on Loch Lomondside

Ghostly gulls in the greyness
keeya, keeya, keeya, keeya
september at Applecross

Tiree
on a march morning
the kingdom of the wind

Seven islands
in the august sunlight
Islay, Jura, Scarba, Lunga, Luing, Shuna, Seil

*

Walking the coast
all those kyles, lochs and sounds

sensing the openness
feeling out the lines

order and anarchy
chaos and cosmology

a mental geography

*

Have you heard Corrievreckan
at the Spring flood
and a westerly blowing?

the roaring's so great
you can hear it twenty miles
along the mainland coast

admiralty charts
show a 9-knot race

to the senses
that do no calculations
but take it all in
it's a rushing white flurry

birthplace
of a wave-and-wind philosophy

*

Let the images
go bright and fast

and the concepts be extravagant
(wild host to erratic guest)

that's the only way
to say the coast

all the irregular reality
of the rocky sea-washed West

*

Pelagian discourse
atlantic poetics

from first to last

TRAIL'S END

1.

Dark waters, home
of greylag goose, blackthroated
diver
salmon, charr and trout . . .
after ten days' drought
the rain has returned
a grey smir
obscuring the loch, smooring
the hills

2.

Chill dawn air
this rock:
those Ice Age markings

3.

Birch grove
silver-blurred in the rain
the bleached trunk
of a dead
pine
deer-print
in the peaty ground

4.

Burn water grey
club moss
tight on the stones
and a single
arctic
black-stamened
white-petalled
flower

5.

Looking down over
the rock and scree
watching a ptarmigan
make it
over the ridge

OUT OF ASIA

SCENES OF A FLOATING WORLD

I.

A warm white mist over the bay
and an old junk making it
the slow way—
something would like this quietness to stay . . .
but already it's day: cranes turning,
people scurrying, engines chugging,
sirens howling, phones ringing
—and Hong Kong wakens to more money-making

2.

Fish market look-see:
the red sun glistens
on big-eyes, bream, manta rays
shark, barracuda, sea-snake
while blue smoke rises from joss-sticks
lit by bone-weary fishermen
in thanks for Queen of Heaven's bounty
and safe home-coming into Fragrant Harbour

3.

Sounds of Cantonese
and a confusion of yellow faces
(Hong Kong side—Kowloon side)
the ferry-boat open to the wind
crosses the green strait
amid junks, walla-wallas, launches:
red and black print of newspaper
and a whiff of the South China Sea

4.

She's a private secretary
('how private', she asked when she got the job)
twenty years old, pretty as a picture (no plastic surgery)
makes about $3 000 (H.K.) a month
has a flat to herself in Happy Valley
mistress to a rich local doctor
and dreams of being a student in Hawaii—
crossing the ferry 'in the morning time'

5.

The old black Mongolian beggar
comes down from his roost
in the Kowloon hills
long-haired, laughing to himself
walking the pavement with naked feet
leaving a trail of emptiness
a long trail of laughing emptiness
that goes back to Cold Mountain

6.

In the airconditioned skyscraper office
a thousand cases of Mexican abalone
come in on one line
and a ton of Chinese rabbits
leave on another—while in the backstreets
old men play noisy mahjong
among the guff of frying titbits, the stench
of decaying vegetables, and the ghostly smell of incense

7.

In his cluttered little premises on Mody Street
Bossie Wong, alias Édouard (British passport, Mauritian French,
     Chinese)
waits for his next batch of clients
ready to supply them with suits, cases, watches—you name it
and offering his famous underworld mystery tour
with flower-boats and darkened omnibus
where you can feel up a nude little neighbour
for so much every five minutes

8.

Lying at his ease
stretched out against a pillar at Kowloon Pier
Ken Cameron, vagrant
opens the *South China Morning Post*
reads the speech made by a British general
at a rotary club dinner—
then turns to the many-dated shipping page
looking for a likely boat

9.

With two new film-scripts under his arm:
'The Canton Killers', 'Murder in Macao'
(guaranteed 100% commercial success)
white-suited moustachio'd Brooklyn Joe
walks up Nathan Road in the blue afternoon
while the young model practises smoking the cigarette
that makes her sick
('We are Hong Kong people, no politics')

10.

Scott Hawkins, writer
having travelled all Asia
sits in his hotel room in Tsimshatsui
a bottle of whisky at his elbow
and a newly bought notebook before him—
on the notebook's first page is inscribed
'The Face of the East Wind'
below that: 'an unwritten novel'

11.

At nightfall, the streets are strident
with neon signs, black
dance of ideograms; a blond-haired Dutch girl
shows clammy breasts to Japanese tourists
in a smoky cellar; a Filipina girl does the same
for beer-happy Yankee sailors
while bulldog British businessman is daintily escorted
by a tongue-tied little Hongkongese

12.

Kowloon Kino:
peeled oranges at the entrance
chestnuts roasting in charcoal
sputtering chicken, meatballs, tripe—
inside the huge hall
your neighbour puffs like a maniac and spits on the stone floor
while bones crunch, blood spurts
and heroines whimper on the giant screen

13.

In his tenth floor flat
in the backlands
laid out Japanese style with mats
but with a Chinese *pi-pa* in one corner
Christopher Cheung
('I am not an artist, I am a human being')
pours himself a glass of *maotai*
and thinks of Kyoto

14.

In the bar near 2 o'clock closing-time
Oscar Eberfeld, bachelor, 46 years old
eyes with hopeless desire
the little slit-skirted serving-girl
follows a wench on the pavement
glued to the knicker-line showing through her pants
then returns unconsoled to his room
with a glossy magazine

15.

Over in Aberdeen
a satisfied rat slides home
under the floor of a waterfront restaurant
the last gamblers yawn and spit
the last sampan putters in to anchorage—
while two heavy-beamed stern-high junks
plough the dark harbour
bound for ancient fishing-grounds

THE EIGHT ECCENTRICS

China, in the Tao times

1.

They say I feed on the wind
and drink dew
that's true—some of the time

but now and again
you'll find me in a village tavern
drinking rice wine
and eating fish
served by a pretty young waitress
then
after taking a good look around
listening to how the people talk
(always the same old crap)
I come back up into the hills

to follow the way of the white clouds

2.

I'm the one does everything all mixed up
and backside foremost

when I go into town
I put a shoe on one foot
and leave the other bare

that gives people a laugh
and gets the conversation going

up in the mountains
I like sprawling naked in the snow
reading the *Autumn Waters*

when the notion comes over me
I get up on the back of a white crane
and do some celestial sight-seeing

if you see what I mean

3.

I used to go
for long walks in the country
thinking about the Way . . .

one day I came across
two old raggedy fellows
who said:
—What do you think you're doing, boy?
—I cultivate the Way
—Where's the Way? they said
I pointed up to heaven
—Where's heaven? they said
I pointed to my heart
they laughed, the two of them
and said:
—OK, come away with us

4.

Property?
ten thousand acres of white cloud
culture and the arts?
the wind in the pines

you can sit on a cushion and meditate
till you're blue in the face
you'll never know the real way of things
when people ask me to explain the Way
I just point to the sun and moon

5.

They say I had a white mule
that could travel a thousand miles a day
which is all baloney

it's true I had a grey mule for a while
but it went to the mules' paradise
before very long
and mostly I went about on foot
like it better that way

people don't really care for the mountain life
prefer security and boredom
so they sit at their hearths
and make up stories
to make it all sound marvellously impossible

6.

I was making for the capital
to sit the civil service exam
when I had that dream

I'd come out well
I had an important post
I had a wife and a son and a daughter
then my wife took a lover
war broke out
my son was killed my daughter carried off
I had to take to the hills
living on nothing

when I woke up
I decided I might as well
come up into the hills right away

so I did
and this unofficial existence
suits me down to the ground

I prefer pinetrees to politicians

7.

As a young man they told me
I'd better undertake some serious studies
I told them I didn't want to study
all the dreary stuff they went in for
and I wrote them this poem:

'I'll live in the woody mountains
in a cave beside a waterfall
I'll play the Green Jade Song
on a seven-stringed lute
I'll grow a magic mushroom or two
and feed them to a snow-white crow'

I've lived like that
for close on fifty years
now I'm lying here under a pure autumn sky
with a smile on my face

8.

I never wanted to be president
of the company, or the country
I wanted to be what I read in the old books
'a real man without situation'

you don't often come across fellows like me
here today and gone tomorrow
following the ten directions of the heart

home for me is a hillside cave
out on one of the Eastern Islands
don't think I live a sad life there
I drink white wine and let my soul
fly about with the gulls

THE HOUSE OF INSIGHT

> *Developing insight is like diving*
> *into the deep waters of sensation*
> Nagasena, *Vipassana*

I saw myself disappearing
and it was good
for I was still there
another

eliminate the intermediary me

I was Gauguin
I was a Chinese scholar

totally relaxed
plenitudinous reality

taking off the clothes of the mind
and making love
to the body of reality

entering the stream

void means
beyond the subject-object cage

to be alive
to all the implications
see into the complexity

touching the keys of memory
very solid

re-membering
getting it all together

exciting insighting

the lovely news
the loveliness

a girl blushing
in the metaphysics class

marvellous movements
all kinds of
marvellous movements

that's the girlingest thing
I've ever seen

she's there

taking on the form of a Chinese girl
a German girl, a French girl, an Indian girl

oh girl bellygirl lovely brightmoving girl

coming
always coming
and be-coming

you think it's over
another lovely wave comes

undisturbed
the secret sequence

physics of being
physics of writing
all one

words
like 'em, lick 'em, lip 'em

suck valley dark furry valley
dark furry flurry
slick lick
slit little slit soogling so sucking
lubbery lips lipping

to be into something
ingoing knowing

combinations
aware of 'em happening
with all my senses

red rut in the golden body
dark in the gold
raw red in the dark gold

making love to the unknown

salmon in the falls
the long green moss caress
the fur-patch touch

did that fellow know what he was saying?
know thyself

silky emptiness
silky silky emptiness

knowing things in the deep pleasure-core

a wet day in the woods
with all senses flush

whale thing pring sling
pale slap slip
spill spale swale whale

a whole white space
we haven't got into yet
the white of a milky wave

everything so absolutely
beautifully clear

beyond images
the fire-body
live from the fire-body

never mind subject object
get into the rhythm

polyrhythmic delight
nothing to do with music
music only makes a noise about it

something else
trying to light up
at the back of my skull

getting down to the wave and pulse level

maybe deep down
we live this way all the time
but we don't know it
our consciousness isn't alive to it

our consciousness
is full of social noise

I could probably invent a mathematics
but my mind is in love
with another kind of truth

the flow doesn't really want
philosophies or science
it wants you
to get into the flow

stop worrying at the world

all those dogmas
all that back-biting
all that anxiety

ah!
the long morning of the mind

smoke dancing
birds flying
river flowing

seeing into it
and feeling it all out

there's no essence
only multi-movement

swirling joyance

she-territory
wave-world

moving among the unnamed

in-being
fields of in-being

no wishful thinking

philosophy's holiday
an ontological vacation

no paradise
but to move in a multiple
paradoxical field

glow-flow

silent

listen

two powers meeting
smile at each other

sun rising
over white flesh ridge
rain of golden fire

fire-body
not the old doll
in the conceptual dustbin

eroto-logic

that's very neat
came to me straight from the Paraclete

multiple meditations
the wonderful understanding
wunderstanding

into the nakedness
behind the signs

deep deep down
where it all
ultimately matters

anonymous conscience
nonymous contact

body-mind beautiful

two jumps ahead
and lightning in the brain

surrounded by eternity

MAHAMUDRA

*When the wind finds no place to stop,
that is* mahamudra.
Mahamudrapadesha

I.

Northwards again
'you come and go, you come and go'
red leaves along the waterways
quiet walking in the rain

feeling your body
growing out of the rain

then into the museum

my ten cents in the machine
the raga mingling with the rain

ah, now

your body in the dance
the red mark on your brow

2.

Out of India
'beautiful as a mare from Kashmir'

eyes like silver fish
long crowblack hair
firm dark round breasts

and the navel's lonely pool

all that I knew of India
all that I knew
centred in your body

surasundari

realising the wave
beyond the ambiguities of love

3.

For years you had followed your path
and I mine
(mine the more erratic—
but *pratyatmavedaniya*
'left to individual')
you with a master
me with a madness

'how can men of this age
of restless mind and lax intelligence
prone to distraction
attain to purity of disposition'

the search among books
the moments the flashes
the encounters

seeing in every girl *prajna*

the one aim: *samarasa*
achieved through aimlessness

4.

Glasgow:
incandescent limbo

in my student's room
listening to India through the wall
(three engineers from New Delhi
modern discs spin for hours on end
smell of smoke-perfume in the hall)
waiter in the Tajmahal:

'my soul is shaking in my belly . . .
my heart is anxious . . . for my girl
who plays . . . the flute'—
kitsch out of Bombay
1960

on the suspension bridge
at twilight
the blue sari

5.

With the word-master in Paris
'useless conversations'
the Bamboo Grove

'le Zen c'est de la connerie
mais les Shingon
ça c'est des gars carabinés'

lodging Rue des Ecoles
ten books a week
the ocean of learning

'the white peaks of the Himalaya'

linking it all
to a few root images

all truth ultimately
within the body
the body-mind
word flesh image bone
'the inarticulate heart's true tone'

6.

'As soon as the conscience
is rid of its covering
it stands out naked
and energy shows its essence'

the lotus and the lightning

'just as salt is dissolved in water
so the mind that takes its woman'

in the arms of the knowledge-girl

earth water fire wind
and space too—honour them

'so he comes into relation
with every kind of creature
and knows the path of freedom'

7.

Now the long-hidden Real
within the names and forms

the moment when
twenty thousand breathings
reach their plenitude

'rain also is of the process'

and the music
and the dancing body

abhisambodhi

it all whirls incessantly

under the laws of change
but there is light in it

there is a rain of light
flooding the brain

'a pure flow of consciousness
a stream of colourless emotion'

PYRENEAN
MEDITATIONS

THE MASTER OF THE LABYRINTH

1.

'I ride in my car
I think of prehistoric caves
in the Pyrenees'—
William Carlos Williams
New York State
circa 1920

2.

He went down there
with a smoking torch
down into
the bowels of the earth
with images of deer
bison horses
flickering in his brain
and he painted them
ecstatically
on the sweating rock

3.

The painted cave
apocalypse of the mind

4.

Five deer cross the mountain stream
necks outstretched, antlers
caught in the light
eyes ignoring history
cross the red ochre water
in a morning of time

5.

Apocalypse of the mind

sex orgy
play of energy

6.

The hunched bison
thunderous magnificent flesh
glares
at the little rag-doll
of an ichtyophallic man
while a bird-stick
planted close by
seems to say
    'signed: the shaman'

7.

Those hands, that eye

8.

What went on down there?
what kind of psychomental theatre?

did he smoke weird herbs in the dark?
did he get *stoned*?

9.

Sitting there petrified

body smeared
with ochre and permanganate

gazing at the wall

10.

Then maybe, feeling horny
blowing his semen into
the crannies of the rock

11.

Came out
sniffing the cool air
reassuring all
that reality was solid
right to the centre

he'd fixed it

VALLEY OF BIRCHES

1.

Entering this valley
        is like entering a memory

        obscure the feeling
        of a plenitude lost
        about to be regained

what is this valley
        that speaks to me like a memory
whispering with all its branches
        this november morning?

2.

The wording would have to come from mental territories still unknown to me, like those phrases I sometimes wake with and that delight me with their freshness and their unstrained complexity—as when, only a few days ago, I woke with the words 'Kanaan Ross' in my mind, the strange ambiguity of the name satisfying me, and its linking of North and East. And it is as though I were now myself that Kanaan Ross, walking in this place, with the need to voice it.

3.

I must enter this birch-world
and speak from within it
I must enter into
this lighted silence

contemplation is not enough

never fully realised
without the necessary words

4.

Without the necessary words

but the most needful words
are the rarest

and how can we come to them
maimed as we are

except through
a power that wings us

out of the maze and the din of unknowing
and enables us

to quietly
penetrate the reality—

this is no question
of industry

5.

*And yet all the work, all the research I have done is not irrelevant to
this encounter. For some time now I have been studying, with a rare sense
of recognition, the geography and mytho-poetry of north-east Asia, that
area inhabited by the hyperborean tribes of the Chuktchee, the Buryat,
the Koriak ... Up in those regions, to which I feel a strong attachment,
so strong they must in some sense be 'my* world', *the birch-tree is
sacred. Indeed the birch-tree is to the North-East what the bamboo is to
countries farther south: the very heart of a culture. It is the birch-culture
at the back of my mind that has given rise to my fascination with this
birch-wood here this morning. Like any complete culture, the birch-culture
links sexuality (for the Siberian tribes the tree is the forest-girl) with
the furthest reaches of the mind. Hence too the plenitude felt by me
earlier, and which I maintain now deep in the dark, protecting it as it
were with this prose periphery, like a bark ...*

6.

Waiting for the words
to come out of the silence

words for this emptiness-plenitude
this absence-presence

words for the sensual spirit
infusing those trees

words like the *nichtwesende wesenheit*
of Meister Eckhart

words like the buddhist *sunyata*
but more rooted, more rooted

rooted and branched
and running with sap

7.

'No people knows now the sensual language', writes Jakob Böhme.
Victims of concept and model, our subtle life flattened under the weight
of the general, we move in sterile worlds, doing violence to everything,
including ourselves. Before we can ever say anything, anything at all, we
must link ourselves, by a long silent process, to the reality. Only long
hours of silence can lead us to our language, only long miles of strangeness
can lead us to our home.

8.

Rain falls from the blue immensities

9.

I have come in under the trees
making love to them with my inarticulate hands

for the beauty at least may be sensed

I have traced out the black on the white
like an unfinished poem—

always broken off, always recommenced

READING HAN SHAN
IN THE PYRENEES

1.

The disciples of Buddha
called him 'poet-monk'
those of Lao-Tzu called him
'hermit and mystic'
and the Confucianists said he was
a crazy eccentric
who sometimes talked sense

for himself
he was just Cold Mountain
doing his best
never knowing exactly
where it was leading him

2.

Du Guangting (850-933)
in his *Shanxian Shiyi*
says Han Shan
'lived on Mt Cuiping
in the Tiantai Mts'

for the Taoists
the Tiantai range
was one of those places
'where men grow wings'

every now and then
he'd go down to the Guoqing monastery
to get food from the kitchen
but mostly he was up there
among the white clouds

3.

Hadn't always been there though
talks of Red Sparrow Street
in Chang'an
where he must have raised the dust
(memories of sweet little girls:
'young girls playing in the twilight
the breeze blows their perfume over the road')
before making for the heights

4.

An unorthodox character
outside the classifications
he'd do a little zazen when it suited him
but made fun of the 'straight backs'
and 'shaven pates' in general

tao-buddhist, okay
but let's just say
mountain-poet
and get into the poems

all three hundred and eleven of them

5.

'A certain smart alec by the name of Wang
said my poems were all wrong
and that I had no sense of prosody
they make me laugh with their "correct" poetry
it's just blind men singing about the sun'

let me find one man with clear eyes
said Han Shan
and my poems will go round the world

6.

'I sauntered off to see a great monk
misty mountain, mile after mile
the old fellow showed me the way back home:
the round lamp of the moon'

'strolling about on Huading Mt
sky clear, marvellous day'

'when the moon's bright
and all white
you can forget about East and West'

7.

Those Cold Mountain poems
are like a day with two dawns

MOUNTAIN STUDY

I.

Why does one study?

for the white-gathered element—
having shaken the letters
to become unlettered

living
in the unlettered light

2.

Every now and then
I go up into the mountains:
fire and snow—
trudging for hours
along the black line of the river
following it right to the crest
or, when the snow's gone
moving up through the forest
to the thin grass and the rocks
the high country—
up there in the stillness
thinking of nothing
only the body moving

3.

Extraordinary ontological territory

4.

Or in my study
with the books of calligraphy
drinking tea or white wine and slowly
leafing through the pages:
Song of the Diaphanous Mirror
Thousand Character Essay
Account of the Retreat of Quietude
The Pavilion of the Drunken Old Man
Treatise on Understanding . . .

5.

But the finest piece of calligraphy
I've ever set eyes on
(back a few years on Taiwan)
is a letter of thirty characters
written by Wang Hsi-chih
in a tough winter of the 4th century
to a good friend of his
asking him how he was faring
in these cold days
a piece of calligraphy which
under the title of
'Clear Sky Just Before Snow'
changed hands for a thousand years
each of its possessors
renaming his study in its honour
so that for a thousand years
somewhere in China
there was a 'Just Before Snow' study

6.

If I named this study of mine
after the pair of scrolls
hanging there on the wall:

seven
mile
stream
shine
bright
outside

ten
thousand
hills
autumn
view

it would have to be something like
The Study of the Seven Mile Stream
or
The Study of the Ten Thousand Hills

7.

In the Study of the Ten Thousand Hills
reading:
'Those who know truth
are not the equals
of those who love it
and those who love it
are not the equals of those
who take active delight in it'

8.

Also writing:
all morning
this quiet thing happening
taking shape, unshaping, reshaping
between me, the language
and the snow
trying adjectives, so many adjectives
running through verbs
(a fine flurry of verbs)
what name for it all, now
midday, and
so little left, only
cool—stillness—soft
drifting—glow . . .
when, opening a Chinese grammar
(red binding still holding
the smell of Glasgow)
my eyes fall on *ta yü hsüeh:*
great rain snow

9.

Movements in the snowy silence
what that line is
and this
no concern now with sense
only a calligraphy
a nameless and meaningless writing
to say without saying
the flurried fullness of
the inner murmuring of
the snowy silence

THE RESIDENCE
OF SOLITUDE AND LIGHT

1.

Suddenly I *see* my table
this table I've worked at
for the past nine years
with the copper lamp
the papers under stones
the bamboo vase of pens and pencils
on the wall beside it
a page of Chinese seals
and the photo of a naked *yakshi*
at the Eastern gate of Sanchi

2.

For nine years my horizon
has been these blue ridges:
this morning snow-scattered
early October—
'autumn hills
here and there
smoke rising'
(Blyth quotes Gyôdai
and refers to Turner)

3.

Books come in through the post:
Studien zur Geschichte Osteuropas
The Buddhist Sogdian Texts

Alphabetisches Verzeichnis zum Kao Seng Ch'uan
Essays on T'ang Society
Gupta Temple Architecture
Etudes Song
The Magic Oracles of Japan
Cahiers du Pacifique
Die Inseln des Stillen Ozeans
Discourses on the Vigyana Bhairava Tantra
Contributions to the Anthropology of Nepal . . .

4.

Working and reworking
the same texts
over and over again
losing all sense
of 'production' and 'publication'
and 'furthering one's reputation'
engaged rather in something
outside literature
that might rightly be called
poetic yoga

5.

Fascinated
by Valéry's analytical geometry of the mind
by Chao's discovery of Buddhism
by the grammars of Khalil and Panini
the drawings of Sesshu
the yoga of Patanjali:

a notion of psychophysical economy
making clean gestures
in clarified space

6.

Like Valéry
saying over and over to myself
beata solitudo
sola beatitudo
but enjoying also
unlike that purest of pure intellectuals
(though he too had his '*long regard*')
enjoying almost mindlessly
the solar field
out there this October morning:
golden sun diffused through mist

7.

Thinking
of Khalil's definition of reality:
$A + A - A - A + A - A + A \ldots$
maybe that's what I've been working at
these last nine years
the result being:

—a pleasant sensation of nothingness-potential
a breathing space
the beautiful breast of emptiness

THE ATLANTIC
MOVEMENT

THE WESTERN GATEWAYS

Prologue

From a crystal window at Saint-Jean-de-Luz
I look out on the Western Seas

listening to the winds:
enbata, the sea breeze
ipharra, the northerner
iduzki-haizea, the wind of the sun
hegochuria, the hot south wind
haize-belza, the dark northwesterly

thinking of the sea of the philosophers
but also of whales and whalemen

I.

Straw fires lit
all along the coast

.smoke signals

drums beating and voices shouting
'baleak berriz etorri dira!'
(the whales are back)

quick, the harpoons

boats out from Biarritz
Socoa and Guéthary

strike!

hauling in the great fat monsters

blood baths, piles of blubber

whale tongue broiling and sizzling
in the little houses of Bayonne

2.

They'd turn up in the Gulf
about the time of the autumn equinox
and were plentiful from January to May

not sperms, or big blues
but the *baleine franche*
the *baleine des Basques*

what the Basques themselves called *sardaka*
and the Hollanders *nord-kapper*

balena borealis

3.

Many a fisherman's cottage
along that basque and gascon coast
had whale bones for rafters

if you lay to rest under such a roof
you saw whales in your sleep!
and when you woke
there were whales in your prayers:

Que Diou ens préserbi
dou cantic de la sirène
dou coudic de la balène
et dou clouché de Mimizan

4.

Came a day
when the whales no longer appeared in Biscay
(because they'd got wise to the Basques
or because of some cosmic change
that had nothing to do with men?)

at Guéthary, they waited
at Bayonne, Biarritz and Saint-Jean-de-Luz
but the whales stayed away

nothing to do but go after them

5.

A hundred boats left every year
every year in the month of March
they'd set out from the Biscay harbours

by April-May they were off the Labrador

Vrolicq of Saint-Jean-de-Luz
drew a map of 'Arctic France'
marking the hunting grounds:
Cap de Biscaye, Baie des Basques . . .

one big fish after another
got a kiss from a Basque harpoon

they built ovens on the beaches
melted down the tons of fat
loaded it into sturdy barrels
and brought it all back home

6.

Other peoples got into the act

like the Bretons of Saint-Malo
Paimpol and the Ile de Bréhat

men from Le Havre and La Rochelle
Dutchmen, Englishmen, Russians, Danes

but if you were after a firstrate harpooner
you still went down to the South-West

the Whaling Company of London
had a recruiting agent at Saint-Jean-de-Luz
the Dutchman Van Muyden, alias Le Flamand
hired twelve Basque sailors at Saint-Jean
including three harpooners

when the *Elizabeth*, captain Jonas Poole
and the *Mary Margaret*, captain Steven Benet
sailed from Liverpool in 1612
they had six Basque harpooners on board:

Jean de Bacogne
Juan de Aguerre
Martin de Karre
Marsine de Horisada
Domingo de Sarria
Adam de Belloka

wild men, every man jack of them

wasn't it said a Basque harpooner
would take a leap on to the whale's broad back
to make sure the dart was well lodged?!

7.

Cleirac, *Us et coutumes de la mer*
describes the harpoon:

'*grand javelot de fer battu
emmanché sur un bois très solide
à la pointe acérée et tranchante
triangulaire en fer de sagette
portant gravée au bout haut
la marque du ministre*'

I saw one years ago in a Dutch museum
the name it bore was
Michelanz de Cubibure
(which must be Ciboure)

8.

Were there any philosophical whalemen
on the misty coasts of America?

Williams (William Carlos) evokes
'the raw beauty of ignorance
that lies like an opal mist
over the West coast of the Atlantic
beginning at the Grand Banks
and extending into the recesses of our brains'

did any of those wild men feel this?

or were they only concerned
with heaving their heavy harpoon
and melting down that bubbling blubber?

some of them must have felt it
even if they couldn't say it

9.

They sang songs:

Pour la grande pêche baleinière
Et pour la chasse aux cachalots
Ont signé l'rôle au commissaire

Vingt-cinq lascars, fins matelots
Sont descendus tous en troupeau
Aux maisons closes d'la rue Rouleau
. . .
Avez-vous vu dans Rotterdam
Écoutez bien c'que j'vas vous dire
La belle Annie qui fut ma femme
Et m'a damné pour son sourire
　　　Embarque le mou au galant
　　　Car la barque roule au vent
. . .
En revenant de La Rochelle
Pique la baleine, joli baleinier
J'ai rencontré Mam'zelle Hélène
Pique la baleine, joli baleinier
Allons naviguer . . .

10.

I imagine a silent harpooner
(his mates think he has no fun)
taking it all in

he sees the white fat in the whale's great brain
he sees the she-whale's milk
thick as mayonnaise

he watches the blue mists rolling on the Labrador

he listens to the Indians talking
and the Eskimo talking
using a kind of pidgin basque

he feels the hugeness of it all
and the grotesque reality of it all

he lives with the vision and the savour of it all

(his mates think he has no fun)

11.

Strange memories lurk in his skull

and when he looks at the Milky Way
he sees ancient pilgrimages

all the starry places along the Pyrenees

Venus advancing along the way
more and more naked with every step

taking the soul to the white lands
gate after gate

seven gates in all
the way of the wild geese

he cannot get it all into focus
but those strange memories go with him

12.

I imagine him also
(oh, he is a strange one)
burning the midnight oil
(a fat candle of whale fat)
and poring over Seneca
(he learned Latin, for fun
from a priest in Bayonne):

'a day will come
when men will find
the great secret hidden in the ocean'

these words he underlines
thinking

13.

Hey, down there
she blows!

blow! blow!
blow! blow!

boats out

quiet
she sounds

quiet

quiet

stand up!

strrrike!

LABRADOR

In the saga times

1.

Another dawn
out from Greenland
whales bellowing in the icy sea
and the vast sky
resounding with wind

once more I felt that breadth of mind
like being drunk
but this was colder and more clear
than anything
that might come out of a jug
it was what I'd always lived for
what I always *will* live for
till they throw me
into the trough of the waves
I was used to dance over

there are those who delight
in the storm of swords
and those who make
public speech with words
these are the warriors and the governors
I have preferred other ways
the lonely ways of the sky of sands
the gull path

in all my lonely ongoings
I have thought of many things
I have thought of the earth
in its beginnings
when time was a sequence of cold dawns

and space was full of
the wings of hallucinated birds

I have dreamed of a primal place
a place of rocks, quick streams and emptiness
each morning
the sun rising in the chill sea of the East
and throughout the long day throbbing
above the rocks, above the waters

the earth then was a nameless place
I have been in love with nameless places
now there are too many names
Norway of the blue streams
is rank with names
the Hebrides and even Greenland
names, names, names
and a welter of angry clamorings—
it was time to move farther West

and so another dawn
out from Greenland
and still no other land in sight
only the green waves and the wind
and a vision strong in the mind

2.

I also named a place
a place of great rocks
and the sun glinting on them
a place filled
with a rush and a flowing of waters
I called it *The Marvellous Shore*

I lived a winter there
it was a time of white silence
I carved a poem on the rocks
in praise of winter and the white silence
the best runes I ever cut

men with long eyes and high cheek-bones
came to visit me
I gave them cloth
they gave me skins
there was peace between us

when Spring came
all the streams running with light
and the big river reflecting the sky
I travelled farther South
into a land of forest
I met red men there
dressed like birds

I was aware of a new land
a new world
but I was loathe to name it too soon
simply content to use my senses
feeling my way
step by step into the reality

I was no longer Christian
nor yet had I gone back to Thor
there was something else
calling to me
calling me out
and waiting, perhaps, to be called

something sensual
and yet abstract
something fearsome and yet beautiful

it was beyond me
and yet
more myself than myself

I thought of talks in Norway
the talk of poets and of thinkers
I thought of high talk in the Hebrides

here was no place for Christ or Thor
here the earth worked out its destiny
its destiny of rocks and trees
and sunlight and darkness
worked out its destiny in silence
I tried to learn
the language of that silence
more difficult than the Latin
I learned in Bergen
or the Irish in Dublin

3.

A whole new field
in which to labour and to think
and with every step I took
I knew a singular health
mind every day more sharp, more clear

I hazarded some more names
(after weighing them carefully each one
trying them out in my mind
and on my tongue):
Great Whale River, Eskimo Point
Indian House Lake, Caribou Pass

but still no name for the whole
I was willing to name the parts
but not the whole

a man needs to fix his knowledge
but he also needs an emptiness
in which to move

I lived and moved
as I had never done before
became a little more than human even
knew a larger identity

the tracks of caribou in the snow
the flying of wild geese
the red Autumn of the maple tree
bitten by frost
all these became more real to me
more really me
than my very name

I found myself still saying things like
'at one with the spirit of the land'
but there was no 'spirit', none
that was outworn language
and this was a new world
and my mind was, almost, a new mind
there was no such thing as 'spirit'
only the blue tracks in the snow
the flying of the geese
the frost-bitten leaf

religion and philosophy
what I'd learned in the churches and the schools
were all too heavy
for this travelling life
all that remained to me was poetry
but a poetry
as unobtrusive as breathing
a poetry like the wind

and the maple leaf
that I spoke to myself
moving over the land

I am an old man now
an old man very old
I have scratched these runes on a rock
to be my testament
perhaps no one will read them
and that is no matter
they will stand on the rock
beside the scratchings of the ice
open to wind and weather

IN THE NASHVAK NIGHT

A summer night on the Labrador
in the twilight watching countless birds
settled and asleep
only a few still on the wing—
that passing flight of Sabine Gulls

is this a death
or the prelude to another life?
the question is all too heavy
breenges into this rippling silence
like a bull into china
better simply to wait
taking pleasure in the twilight

tongues of water
tongues of water from the Labrador
running up the bays and fiords
lapping against the archaean rocks
will say the poem beyond the questioning

the birds are asleep
geese, duck, brant, deal, plover
all are asleep
as though this land were one great sanctuary

here
half-way between the Old World and the New
a stepping-over place
a place to rest
on the long trail of the migrations
North-South, East and West

a place to rest
and yet I am restless
walking here in the stillness

walking in the stillness
half-way between the Old World and the New
trying to move in deeper
ever deeper
into a white world
neither old nor new

white world
neither old nor new
the bird path
feeling it out

dawn comes
with the cry of the wild goose

                              Nashvak Bay, Labrador

BRANDAN'S LAST VOYAGE

1.

Entendez ci de saint Brandent
Que fu nez devers occident
Que VII ans erra par la mer
Por plus douter Dieu et amer . . .

2.

It was a stony kingdom
on the West coast of Ireland
with the wind wailing
and the roaring of Atlantic breakers
with strange men wandering and murmuring:
is é mo drui Crist mac Dé
'my druid is Christ the son of God'

3.

One had always wished to wander farther
Brandan by name and a name it was
that had the sea in it,
the breaking of waves and the memory of a poem
the old men would speak on winter nights:
'Bran thinks a great marvel it is
to sail a boat on the clear sea
Bran's eyes see the waves of the sea
the sea waves shine in summer
as far as the eyes of Bran can see
Bran loves to look upon the sea
the white sea broken by oars . . .'

4.

There are men who are always ready
to throw everything to the winds
men who can look on life coldly
and stake everything on a gesture
Brandan was one of those
God for him was the great gesture
that had set everything in motion
also a great idea sailing through space
brighter than the sun and the moon

5.

Brandan built him a boat

he built it of seventeen places
making first a framework of pliant wood
covering it with bull hides tanned in oak
smearing the hides with grease and resin—
a boat light as a bird to ride the sea!

when the boat was ready, firm and true
he gathered men about him, saying:
'this will be no pleasure cruise
rather the wildest of wild goose chases
around the rim of the world and farther
a peregrination in the name of God
and the promise of white martyrdom'

6.

They pulled away from Ireland, heading North
oars dipping into blue water
amid a caterwauling of gulls

the going was good and the rhythm sure

to the East was the land of the white hills
and they passed by Islay, and the Isle of Tiree
then Barra, the Uists, till they came to Lewis

at the isle of Lewis they went ashore
walked round the ancient stones of Callernish
then headed again for the open sea

7.

The weather went grey and the sea grew gurly
long days of rain, snow, sleet and wind
(surely this must be the very mouth of hell)
Brandan at the prow, crying into the greyness
is é mo drui Crist mac Dé!
the words lost in the grey wastes

never letting up his holy chanting
he kept his eyes skinned for another island

8.

Brandan's mind was full of islands
he had been born and raised among islands
the Hebrides he knew by heart
the Orkneys and the Faeroes too

the world for him was all islands
and weren't the heavens themselves so made?

he was looking for an island now
but so far North he'd never come
the world here was at an end
here there was only sea and wind

at length he let loose one of his crows
and the crow made straight for the Island of Birds

Ka! kaya gaya! keeya! keeya!
branta branta! branta branta!
graak! graak! graak!

that island was noisier than a church
all the birds of the ocean had foregathered there
gulls and redshanks and cormorants
kittiwakes, terns and guillemots
geese and gannets and skuas
some perched on pinnacles of rock
others flying wildly about
ah, it was a goodly sight
and music in Brandan's ears

they pulled up the boat on the bit of beach
and turning it into a shelter
settled down for the night

10.

When Brandan awoke in the morning
he was looking a skua in the eye
and it looked for all the world
·like his old teacher, Mernok
away back there in Munster

'Excuse me, Skua', he said, 'can you tell me
how far we are from Paradise?'

the skua gave a sturdy beat of its wings
and stalked silently off
'I thought so', said Brandan

11.

Ah, it was beautiful, the northern blue
and the clear white curling of the surf!
every mile was a broad blue page of vellum
and Brandan was working out the words

he thought in Latin and he thought in Gaelic
murmuring *'farspag'*, *'in deserto'*, *'muir'*
trying for a freshness never found before

Brandan the voyager would be Brandan the poet
only if he could write a poem
brighter and stronger than all other poems
a poem full of the rough sea and the light

oh, the words for it, the words for a dawning!

to build a boat is good
to sail the faraway seas is good
but to write a poem on which
the minds of men could sail for centuries
that was his ambition now
with a long lifetime behind him

12.

'*Brandanus laboriosus*' they had called him
when he was a busy abbot of monasteries
true, he had always worked like ten
Brandan the Worker, Brandan the Mariner
he had his reputation, sure
but he'd felt it over there on Iona
when he'd been in talk with that Columba
the one who spouted poetry like a book
that somehow he was out beyond the pale
beyond the pale of the literary folk
lacking their polish, their finesse

Columba the Dove and Brandan the Crow

well, it wasn't polish and finesse he wanted
it was a freshness and a force
and a beauty that they'd never know!

13.

Farther and farther they pulled away
into the white unknown . . .

MELVILLE AT ARROWHEAD

The *White Whale* hadn't made much headway
neither had *Mardi*
as for the *Ambiguities*, it was a total flop
and there was nothing more to be hoped for from Hawthorne

So he'd retired to the country:
'a supernatural retreat'—
sitting smoking by the chimney
thinking
with always that sense of immensity
and the physical-metaphysical thing
still raging in his brain
(but he'd try and take it easy)

He liked it best
when the snow piled up at Arrowhead
that removed any temptation
to try and go somewhere else
(sure, his wife pestered him a little
he should take this pill or that pill
which would be good for him
and his daughters, well
they were pleasant enough young ladies
but what could they know
went on back of his blue eyes)
sitting there by his chimney
raising smoke-screens
and thinking of impenetrable Japans

Now and then he'd get up
and finger some object
the head of a harpoon maybe, a piece of ivory
that red back of a crab
picked up on the beach at Nuku-Hiva
or else he'd look at some map
its worn red and yellow and blue
and the ocean currents
would be flowing again through his veins

(a white path in a green sea
a quiet lagoon
a spouting of blood
masses of blubber
and Plato's ghost in the fo'c'sle)

What could any citizen
know about his questing?
what could any parlour poet
know about white whales
or unmapped archipelagoes?

Forget them
life wouldn't last long anyway
soon his bones
would be joining the snow in the Berkshires
and the red leaves
in the Autumn woods
never had any regrets

But that brain of his kept working
beyond all simple wisdom:
grappling with uncouth cosmologies
groping along endless blind alleys
as though nothing could ever please it
but the vision of some unheard of poet

'Herman! supper is ready!'

FIRST SKETCHES OF THE ISLES OF AMERICA

Do you know Macouba?

1. *Manoir de Beauregard*

Lying on the
mahogany-pillared bed

reading Labat's *Journey
to the Isles of America*

while the tropical rain
pours down, pours down
over flame-tree, devil-bell, hibiscus

and the frogs raise their evening chorus

2. *Salines, in the silence*

A grove of curved palms

light wind
swaying the fronds

time here is before
ideas were found

and space wants no sharp lines

3. *Daybreak on the Caravelle*

The outboardmotor skiffs
have skimmed their white way
to the fishing grounds

lights go out one by one
from the houses in Tartane

now watch the magnificent frigates
as they wheel, swoop and wheel
in the bluebright morning

4. *In the restaurant at St Pierre*

After a plate
of lentils and rice

gazing through the window
at the diamonding sea

while the old stones of St Pierre
sleep in the sun

and the servant-girl
seems not to know
how beautiful she looks

5. *Carbet*

Here is where he really learned colour

had come from the Panama
tired out, sick

but he painted
he, and Laval

they painted, drank rum
talked
painted, talked
drank rum

five months later, went home

filled with a dream

6. *Animal kingdom*

The mongoose
noses out, has a keek
then streaks back into the bush

the lizard
head raised, all attention:
little green yogin

7. *In the mangrove swamp*

Root breeding root

only a snake
could find his road
hereabout

Euclid, in this place
would go mad
and Aristotle
take to the bottle

but wait
it'll all work out

8. *Mt Pelée*

There it rises
incredibly clear

like some serene Fuji
in the after-storm air

9. *Fort-de-France, dusk*

A redhaired Negro
dances on the Savane
while his friends look on
laughing, clapping

Hôtel Lafayette, Hôtel Malmaison

the swashbuckling statue
of the founding father
fades away in the dark

what bird has loosed its cry
in the emptiness of the bay?

Martinique, that August

THE HOUSE AT THE
HEAD OF THE TIDE

THE OCEAN WAY

Travelling up the coast
that brightblue Autumn morning
with a head full of Irish whisky
(a certain drunkenness makes thought come easy)

'what matters', I was saying to myself
'nothing human, that's sure'

it was one of those supernihilistic journeys
only an extravagant Scot
or maybe a Greek or a Russian
can know

'*bonjour, beauté*', I said
in passing, to the world

sea-cloud in the sky

ozeanisches Gefühl

Bordeaux
Bourse maritime, Dansk Konsulaat
Bar de la Gironde, Le Tampico, Atlantic Bar

a whiff of dark-red wine

and the big river
mother-of-waters
flowing slowly West
in a golden haze

MAMAN ROSE
FOIE GRAS

farewell to Gascogne

it was September
red apples
all along the road

night gathering
the waves darkening

kingfisher!

a round white moon
over La Rochelle

on the Place de l'Ancre
an electric guitar
and a slim girl singing
L.A. Woman

wind in the tamaris
cool wind in the tamaris

'Don't bogart that joint, my friend
pass it over to me'

red lamp out on the harbour waters

next morning
the flat lands of Vendée
low houses, marshes
fish, oysters, salt
white wind
white light

'what whiteness
will you add to this whiteness?'

high bridge over the Loire
at Saint-Nazaire

CHANTIERS DE L'ATLANTIQUE

La Roche-Bernard:
a full-sailed yacht
coming silently down the Vilaine
between the steep rock banks

eros, logos, cosmos

Armorican territory
the dumnonian coast

a sea-shaken house

salutations to Duns Scot
Scotus Erigena
and old Pelagius

vita maxima contemplativa

at the swirling centre
fire-wave, lightning-flower

BROKEN ODE TO WHITE BRITTANY

And we're out
once again
on the transhuman road

. . .

A nation?
a county?

broken coastlines

here
no one talks
about states

. . .

'Dull weather,' they tell me
they don't hear the gulls laughing whitely

. . .

Brest
midnight
in the Dead Man's Bar:

'another shot of that lousy red!'

. . .

Suddenly
here I am
in the Glasgow Road

and three mad ghosts
walking by my side

. . .

Introduced as a poet
he talked supernihilism

. . .

Down by the harbour:

sun-
light playing on the prow
of the *Agios Ioannis*, Famagusta

. . .

Anonymous archipelago

blue breakings

confused clarities

. . .

Reading beyond the legends

. . .

Enough
enough of that, enough of those

this wave breaking

white prose

. . .

May it never, don't forget
smell the poet

. . .

At last a little realness
this taste of salt on the tongue

. . .

White mist
at Roscoff

the outgoing tide
at Douarnenez

. . .

When they said: writing
he said: opening

. . .

Write poems?

rather follow the coast
line after line

going forward

breathing

spacing it out

. . .

Geographical calligraphy

. . .

This emptiness
that laughs at everything

all except *that*

. . .

Over against the -logies
of the logos gone dry

those two words!

sunt lumina

. . .

On the ridge of Trévézel

rough grass
black stone

and a clear wind out of the north

. . .

All those
looking for a key

when all the time there's no door

. . .

Lighting up the world
with a white gesture

. . .

At the Pointe du Van
this dawn

brain full of waves

. . .

That
to see it—

getting back into space

. . .

Praise of pelagian space

. . .

Played out
all the dialectics

. . .

Sunday morning at Plouguerneau

a gull crying
over the mass

'When Finn was alive, and the Fianna
moor and sea
meant more than any church'

THE ARMORICAN MANUSCRIPT

1.

Leaving the world
to its bickering and bargaining
he came over to Armor
across miles of metaphor

to the final door

2.

To the East
the rising sun

to the South
red moors

to the West
the great coast

to the North
white fields

3.

Rough rock
in the times of all that
hollow talk
rough rock edges, and
swirling
white sleek water
a wind-water place
with its curves and its cries
ora maritima
estuaries and tides
wings, waves, sands
rain and light

4.

He liked the old tongue
with its rocky sounds:

'*War an dervenn pa bar al loar*
bep noz 'n em zastum evned-mor

Evned-mor du o fluñv ha gwenn
gant ul lommig gwad war o fenn

Ganto ur Vranez gozh du-lovet
ganti ur Vran yaouank kevret

Skuizh o daou ha gleb o eskell
o tonet eus tramor, eus pell

Hag an evned a gan ur c'han
ken kaer ma tav ar mor ledan'

5.

'*Bran*', he thought
looking at the cormorant
drying its wings
in the morning sun
—and it was Megara, that promontory:
marine semantics
thalassic philosophy

6.

He often dipped into the little book
of Marban the hermit:

'Birds come, bright and fair
herons, gulls
it's no sad music
the sea brings here
and brown grouse
out of red heather

noise of wind
through branchy wood
grey cloud, water
falls
cry of swan
fine music'

7.

Out there
no circus

only watching
and listening to the place

far away from noise
and from nuisance

worshipping
monotony and silence

novice of emptiness

8.

Walking deliberately
on the great white beach
he recalled his Latin:

ineffabilis fatus
inaccessibilis accessus
incorporalis corpus
superessentialis essentia
illocalis localitas
infiniti definitio
incircumscripti circumscriptio

'the road to paradise
is paved with paradox'

9.

Out, in clear fact, beyond culture:

chaos surviving
in the rock's red veins
(silent gull
gliding
over thin white sand)

10.

It wasn't his voice
but he liked the old songs
that held the soul of the place:

'The rain is falling
on the Arrée hills
the rain is falling
on the shores and fells

The rain is falling
on Cape Fréhel
the rain is falling
on the woods of Huel

The rain is falling
on the Isle of Ouessant
the rain is falling
on the roofs of Port-Blanc

The rain is falling'

11.

Over on the headland
where the wind, from second to second
turns into light

he felt
a sense of living
at the edge of all knowing

12.

Sometimes
he'd have a crack
with the ancient folk:

'Merlin, old Merlin
where go ye this mornin'
with your holly stick
and your big black dog?

yoo hoo, yoo hoo!

I seek the red egg
of the great sea-snake
I seek the green cress
and the golden grass

yoo hoo, yoo hoo!'

13.

And the crows
those ragged rabbis

told apocalyptic stories
in the beech's branches

14.

He liked the wild tales
that stand on the border
between two worlds:

'Near the forest of Caniscan
lives the hermit Iscolan

Seven years he's been out in the wind
for that he sinned

He sleeps on the barest stone
the poor man, Iscolan

When the grass is alive with fire
it's Iscolan's desire

A little book is all he wants
to be free of those wild haunts

The wee book's in the gob of a cod
that swims deep in the sea of God'

15.

On the hawthorn path
that went down to the bay
(a labyrinth
of glimmer and shade)
he liked to feel
the clarity
gradually unveil—
till it came at him suddenly
with the beat of the wind

16.

The boat he sailed
it was easy to recognize:

that high bow
with very marked sheer
and full-cheeked stem
the peak of the mainsail
high above the mast
boom extending well beyond stern

17.

Sometimes out at sea
he's sing himself a shanty song:

'Sur l'île de Saint-Malo
je connais un matelot
qu'a fait l'tour du monde
de Brest à Bornéo

Sur son bateau la Blonde
il voguait sur les flots
pour faire le tour du monde
d'Moscou à Macao

L'a vu la terre entière
l'a vu le bout du monde
épousé une bergère
sur les îles de la Sonde

A l'âge de cent deux berges
l'est revenu à Saint-Malo
pour rêver à des vierges
d'Oslo, d'Acapulco'

18.

In the blue morning mist
off the coast
that rock the seabirds
had covered
with immaculate shit . . .

he never tired
of watching it

19.

Saying to himself:

where goes the world?
to the white

where goes the white?
to the void

where goes the void?

the void comes and goes
like the light

THE HOUSE
AT THE HEAD OF THE TIDE

Five miles out of town
you come to a place called
the White Field

two wings and a whiteness
(ideogram for 'perseverance')

moorland, a rocky coast
and a hundred islands
the sea often green, gurly green
but every now and then
a sharp, breath-catching blue
with always breakers

peace, peace in the breakers

a place, this, of darkness and of light
darknesses and lights
in quick succession
the sun reveals, cloud conceals
and always a music
of wind on moor, tide on shore
and a silence

a fifth quartet

'we must be still
and still moving
for a further union
a deeper communion
through the dark cold
and the empty desolation
the wave cry, the wind cry
the vast waters
of the petrel and the porpoise'

a country lane lined with gorse
this house of stone
lined with a thousand books
that speak of ideas, islands
according to an order
as yet only dimly apprehended
vaguely sensed

chaoticism

where are we?
where are we going?
one who has thought his way
through the thicket
says it is a question of
moving into a new place
a clearing
we speak here in terms of
atlantica
a breathing and a breadth

pelagian space:
what was left out and behind
when the roads were built
and the codes of command

crammed into the mind
what was left out
becoming more and more
faintly articulate

still there in the gull cry
the wave clash
those darknesses, those lights
(but who hears? who sees?
who can say?)

another mindscape

moving out then
into the landscape
walking
in the white of the morning

walking and watching
listening

yellow flowers
tossing in the wind
a crow on a branch
caw-cawing
the rivulet
reflecting the sky
in blue-grey ripples
white beach, wrack
the high gait and snootiness
of oyster-catchers
a blue crab groping in a pool
bright shell

the notes accumulate

towards a writing
that has more in view
than the art of making verse
out of blunt generalities
and personal complaining

atlantic archipelago
and a sense of something
to be gathered in

the mind gropes
like a blue crab in a pool
tosses in the wind
reflects the sky in ripples
flies high
leaves signs in the sand
lies recklessly strewn
at the edge of the tide

comes back to the books
the many manuscripts

scriptorium
in candida casa
altus prosator

binoculars focused also
on the red-roofed
abandoned sardine-factory
at the tip of the promontory—
some kind of homology

a place to work from
(to work it all out)
a place in which to
house a strangeness

this strange activity
(philosophy? poetry?
practice? theory?)

from an accumulation of data
to the plural poem

beyond the generality

THE CHAOTICIST MANIFESTO

Wave, wind, wing
            plunges
veers
   play and display
        idea-energies
blue, yellow, white
           the light
      changes
    no knowledge, Mister
      only the being there
     outside
      what you were
   a space
        full of events
originary practice
      what?
     words without language
       fragmentary syntax

and yet coherence
chaos-poem
this
that is coming
Ereignis
hah!
watch, listen
white wing
red roof
the writing, the thing
the thing seen, heard
the thing thought
raised
into what
is not metaphysics
but *claritas*
le bel aujourd'hui
they're all here
the thinkers
those of the *Anfang*
writhing in the wrack
wheeling in the light
blowing in the wind
the gathering
colloque de la côte
towards the plural poem
chorus
coruscations
(where's the Chinaman?
up there on the hill
running helter-skelter down to the sea
feng shui)
this is today
raised out of history
the pencil

has been sharpened
                    the eye
has been cleaned
the hand confirmed
        no remains
    economy of presence
here now this
    worked out space
            no scheming
    anarchic
            and yet archaic
(archaic anarchy—
the most beautiful paradox)
                    Pelagius
steps out of a hollybush
            bright!
        Erigena
walks quiet along the shore
        sunt lumina
the mind
            is inspired
the landscape
            enlightened
the mindscape
    exists
            (no reason no anguish)
        who what
without why
    and the questioning
        fresh
    as the cry
of the gull on the headland
                keeya! keeya!
keeya! keeya!
        here at the sea's edge

laughing
    laughing a new laugh
      (quotations, quotations
    at home in this topography
     beyond the nations)
      whiteness
 is what it means
     but a whiteness written
like birch bark
   like wave crest
      with lines and with sound
    original
  (no ideal, no model)
       eventual
     nothing is absent
    and this body-mind
  says it all
      all the ways
  lead to here
     have lead to here
   the sky has broken
   and the earth
     sea-washed
      is all diamond

THE WINTER CEREMONY

1.

It's still dark
with big flakes drifting by the window
and the roofs of the outhouses
are all hump-backed
when I switch on the radio:

'Bréhat semaphor calling
this is the national
weather forecast
for the coastal zone
between Cape Fréhel and Lannion Bay
today, 8th January:
very low temperature
under thick cloud
wind from ten to fifteen knots
calm sea
visibility often less
than one mile
with frequent snow'

The whole department of the Côtes-du-Nord
is absolutely snow-bound
it's been snowing on Ushant
for the first time in a century
here at Gwenved
above Lannion Bay
beside the old sanctuary
there's nothing
no noise
only the grey sky, the blue forest
and the long murmur of the sea

Birds cross the sky now and then
gulls and sterns
and sea-pies
white, white and black in the white
with an occasional thrush or sparrow
brownly fluttering round the threshold
but mostly there's nothing
just the snow falling
and the hum of the heating plant
here in the study

and the white light
the subdued white light
filtering through the snow-covered window

2.

'The myth people
were living at Crooked Beach
the house of the Wolves
stood at the North end of the village
their chief was called
Travelling Wolf . . .'

It's been snowing for two weeks now
off and on, but over two weeks
when the snow's falling, the horizon's grey
when it isn't falling, the horizon's blue
my eyes have got used to this grey-white-blue
to the wind and the silence
to the isolation
it's going to be none too easy
to pick up again with society . . .

3.

I've been reading about the Kwakiutl winter ceremony
(Franz Boas's account)
all the dancing
and the storytelling—
but I prefer by far this quieter thing
outside any community

'His name was Lone Wolf
he went round the world
feeling out the lines of the earth
then he holed up in the snow
remembering
and listening to the snow'

4.

Snow over Europe—
that's the title of some thirties' poem
when a red star shone over China
and Left Book Club editions
stood on the shelves of my father's bookcase
a little last snowy peace
before the big show
(some now I hear are nostalgic
for all that noise
for the beliefs and the counter-beliefs
the stances
and the stanzas
about Glory and Humanity and the Future
along with several other themes
which hopefully by this time
have been lifted by the scavengers)

Let's get into the snow out there

Maybe to start off with
singing a little shaman song
something like this:

'There's a bear's head
and a crow's wing
at my door

I walk between
blue forest
and white shore

nobody knows
what I'm doing here
what I'm looking for'

Are you with me?

5.

'They went down to Seal Coast
the Wolf people
and the Bear people
and the Crows
they went down to Seal Coast
somebody started beating a drum'

The old heron of the Ile Millau
is wrapped in a blue dream
there's a little band of oystercatchers
freezing on the beach of Pors Mabo

I walk along the shoreline in the snow

LATE AUGUST ON THE COAST

Prologue

Ah, the breathtaking beauty of this late August,
now the summer people are gone,
and the beaches silent again—
    great mists rising up over the sea
    and moving inland
    along the little valleys
    (all morning it's a misty world
    a quiet *Niflheim*)
    but by early afternoon
    the mist bank breaks
    now here, now there
    revealing blue-gleaming stretches of water
    a piney wood
    a red fern moor
    a stony village . . .

Rain, tea and a butterfly

    Eight o'clock
    grey sky and a quiet rain
    I want to enjoy (and maybe ingeniously employ)
    long hours of this
    so I've unplugged the telephone
    (ah, this delicious sensation
    of total isolation—I just hope
    no one will turn up spontaneously
    to ask me if I believe in God
    or invite me to come and turn tables
    or tell me about their family squabbles . . .)
    I look around

at a few things I have on the wall:
a 19th century print of a blue rorqual
(1/72 natural size)
stranded on a misty, rocky shore,
a leaf from a zoological album
showing a grey-backed seal
(*pélage moine*
squelette de la tête vu de profil)
and a page out of
Grønlandske Fangere Fortaeller
showing eight fishes of Greenland
from the polar cod, *gadus callarius*
to the sleeping shark, *somniosus microcephalus*
(we whose homeland
is the world
as the sea is to fish
says Dante—
but what's the world?) . . .
the eye moves on to
a Japanese print
'Kambara: snow at night'
and to another
'Sunset on a snowy day at Uchikawa'
I go make some tea
the red earthenware pot
is now there at my elbow
I'll lie out there on the bed
with the Tunisian blanket
(Avicenna, ah, Avicenna)
drink the tea while it's hot
and watch the rain
the quiet-falling rain
through the philosophical window:
there's a butterfly there
some kind of Admiral

(I'm more than a little vague about admirals)
maybe it's old Chuang-tzu
come out of the tea pot
(why not, after all?)
to talk with me about the *tao*:
OK, butterfly, what's the *tao*?
(like, at least grammatically
what's the time?)
flutter flutter, a red flutter-flutter
(I feel my pulse:
the answer to an existential question
can never be mathematical)—
there's Reich and Heidegger walking by'. . .
rain and tea and a butterfly:
do I have here the makings
of a fiction supreme?
will this rainy day
at August's end
give me a new look into reality
or a wonderful waking dream?
I go downstairs
read a page or two of Melville
a page or two of Thoreau
a page or two of *The Oregon Trail*
(I intend some day
to write a series of lectures
on 'American space' and the question of the real
that'll make David Herbert Lawrence and the rest
sound like *Paris-Match* or the *Reader's Digest*) . . .
the butterfly's still fluttering at the window
I pour tea in the cup again
and lie listening to the quiet rain

Epistle to the Birds of this Coast

You gulls who know this coast
from the Aber Wrac'h to the Seven Islands
you of the red-tipped beaks
you terns and kittiwakes
you oyster-catchers
you band of ghostly herons
still holding out on the Ile Millau
(I see you in the evening
over the pine wood
grey-blue in the blue)
this is just to say
I'm glad and grateful that you're there
because if you weren't
if you were all gone
that would mean the others had won
the advancing ones
the constructive ones
with their crazy beliefs and their lousy ideologies
their oil-slicks and their nuclear garbage
their noises and their nuisances
(they don't know how to walk the coast
they have to have all kinds of
games and animations
they don't even know what they've lost)—
so
please keep on using the sky
as you know how
riding the wind
with your eyes wide open
tracing out the shoreline
(along with something else it's harder to define)
and throw out a cry or two now and then
for those of us down here who care

that'll be a kind of reminder
(to accompany the signs
we read silent in the stone):
way beyond the heart's house
right into the bone

The Nameless Archipelago

Out there
nameless
sometimes in certain lights
I think I have it
(that last glance over the coast rocks
in the gathering evening . . .
or in the white mist of early morning)
but there's no exactitude
(I'm not content after all to be a mystic)
at other times I get exactness
but I feel it as fragment
(like picking up a stone
with no sense of geology)
I can sometimes even feel part of it myself
when I'm swimming in the sea
(marine yoga, kind of)
but that's not knowing it
and there's no expression
(I'm not even sure any more what 'knowing' means
and as to expression
I don't just mean poetry
I suppose what I'm after is closer
to a kind of cartography) . . .
in the map room here
looking at the world of
Dionysius Periegetes

(*Celtae, Scythae, mare cronium*)
the periplum of Pytheas up to Thule
a nautical atlas
(Portugee, early 16th century)
of the North-East Atlantic
(*oceanus britannicus, mare iperboreum*)
Al Sharqi's map of the Mediterranean
a Korean map of China and Japan
and a Blue River itinerary . . .
sometimes
maybe to make things easier
I imagine this nameless place
as a bird sanctuary
peopled with creatures whose brains
are less complex than mine
so that for them
everything clicks all the time
(it's true that merely to hear
the cry of some gull on the shore
is enough to awaken—*wakan*—
the old 'metaphysical' desire):
to say it's a sanctuary
is to say it's admirable
but uninhabitable . . .
how to inhabit (intimately)
a place with no name?—
one would have one's-self
to have no name
but if there are no names
what can one say?

The Music of the Landscape

Listening in
(late August morning)
to the music of the landscape:
sea-wind
blowing veil after veil of grey
up the valley of Goaslagorn
flights of wailing birds
over the fields
young birches
with scarcely frosted trunks
rain-whispering
hoarse ragged firtrees on the skyline . . .
along the shore
(all the islands wrapped in mist
but the surf outlines them
with silent thunder)
a restlessness, a movingness
a chaos-noisiness:
unruled masses of sound
interrupted by sharp cries
or a wave breaking
on ice-scored rock
(no place this
for sympathies or symphonies
any kind of easy
harmonisation:
the weather is everchanging
and from Dourven point
to Ploumanac'h's centred complex
the topography abrupt)—
yet there is
something like a music there
in the grey rain

and the sharp cries
and the wind
that travels the changing skies
there is something
immensely
satisfying to the mind
corresponding
to its highest demand:

admitting no simple equations
and laughing at any solemn questions

A Short Introduction to White Poetics

Consider first the Canada Goose
brown body, whitish breast
black head, long black neck
with a white patch from throat to cheek
bill and legs black
flies in regular chevron or line formation
flight note: *aa-honk*
(that's the one old Walt heard on Long Island)

Then there's the Barnacle Goose
black and white plumage
white face and forehead
(in German, it's *Weisswangengans*)
flight in close ragged packs
flight note
a rapidly repeated *gnuk*:
gnuk gnuk gnuk gnuk gnuk gnuk gnuk
(like an ecstatic Eskimo)

Look now at the Brent Goose
small and dark
black head, neck and breast

brilliant white arse
more sea-going than other geese
feeds along the coast
by day or by night
rapid flight
seldom in formation
irregularly changing flocks
her cry:
a soft, throaty gut-bucket *rronk*

The Red-Breasted Goose
has a combination of
black, white and chestnut plumage
legs and bill blackish
quick and agile, this beauty
seldom flies in regular formation
cry:
a shrill *kee-kwa kee-kwa*
(who, what? who, what?)

The Greylag
pale grey forewings
thick orange bill
lives near the coastline
flies to grazing grounds at dawn
usually in regular formation
cry: *aahng ung-ung*
(like a Chinese poet
exiled in Mongolia)

As to the Bean Goose
she has a dark forewing
and a long black bill
talks a lot less than other geese
just a low, rich, laconic *ung-unk*

The Snow Goose
has a pure white plumage
with blacktipped wings
dark pink bill and legs
(in North America turns blue
a dusky blue-grey)
in Europe you might take her for a swan
or maybe a gannet
till she lets you know abruptly
with one harsh *kaank*
she's all goose

so
there they go
through the wind, the rain, the snow

wild spirits
knowing what they know